D1288622

BASIC CONSTRUCTION BLUEPRINT READING

BASIC CONSTRUCTION BLUEPRINT READING

MARK W. HUTH

VNR **VAN NOSTRAND REINHOLD COMPANY**
New York   Cincinnati   Toronto   London   Melbourne

Printed in the United States of America.

Published by Van Nostrand Reinhold Company
A division of Litton Educational Publishing, Inc.
135 West 50th Street, New York, NY 10020, U.S.A.

Van Nostrand Reinhold Limited
1410 Birchmount Road
Scarborough, Ontario M1P 2E7, Canada

Van Nostrand Reinhold Australia Pty. Ltd.
17 Queen Street
Mitcham, Victoria 3132, Australia

Van Nostrand Reinhold Company Limited
Molly Millars Lane
Wokingham, Berkshire, England

16 15 14 13 12 11 10 9 8 7 6 5 4 3 2

Library of Congress Cataloging in Publication Data

Huth, Mark W.
    Basic construction blueprint reading.

    Includes index.
    1. Building—Details—Drawings.   2. Blue-prints.
I. Title.
TH2031.H76   692'.1   79-25438
ISBN 0-442-23874-6

PREFACE

Working drawings are prepared for all construction projects, large or small, new construction or renovation. These drawings are the language by which construction personnel communicate. A thorough understanding of these working drawings provides the basis for further study of construction.

Although working drawings are no longer made by the blueprint process, it has become common to refer to them as blueprints. BASIC CONSTRUCTION BLUEPRINT READING helps you develop the ability to read and sketch construction drawings. The first section discusses the principles of working drawings. This provides the background necessary for further study. The second section covers the elements of sketching in a logical sequence. The ability to sketch is valuable for anyone studying working drawings and for the building trades worker in the field. Section three presents a brief overview of light construction. An understanding of the elements of construction enables you to fully comprehend the discussion of construction drawings in section four.

Each of the units has an assignment involving practical application of the unit's content and questions to measure your comprehension. The assignments in the last section refer to actual drawings and specifications for a small house. These drawings and specifications are packaged in the back of the book. They can be removed for easy reference.

Several individuals and companies contributed to this book. The author is especially grateful to W.D. Farmer, Inc. for permission to adapt their drawings; Richard T. Kreh, Sr. for reviewing the manuscript and offering constructive criticism; and Barbara Brown for copy editing the manuscript.

CONTENTS

Section 1
BASIC BLUEPRINT READING

UNIT 1 INTRODUCTION TO CONSTRUCTION DRAWINGS

OBJECTIVES

After completing this unit, the student will be able to:

- explain the importance of drawings in construction.
- describe the methods of reproducing drawings.

THE IMPORTANCE OF DRAWINGS

The construction of a structure involves many people working at different locations. Architects and engineers design the project, bankers and the owner finance the job, and building trades workers construct it. Each of these groups needs to communicate with the others. Construction drawings are used for this communication.

As the design professionals — the architects and engineers — develop their design, they make rough notes and sketches. Drafters prepare working drawings from these notes and sketches. These working drawings give information about the size, shape, and location of all parts of the structure to others involved with the project, figure 1-1, page 2.

In order to insure that these drawings will be interpreted the same by everyone who reads them, rigid rules are followed. Such things as the weight of lines, the location of dimensions, and the position of the views can affect the meaning of a drawing. To read and understand construction drawings accurately, it is important to understand these rules.

DRAWING REPRODUCTION

When the drafter in the architect's or engineer's office completes a set of working drawings, copies must be made to give to all necessary personnel. The original working drawings are stored in the architect's or engineer's office for future reference. Making these copies is called *reproduction*. Drawing reproduction can be done in several ways and may include enlarging or reducing the size of drawings. This unit discusses only the most commonly used methods.

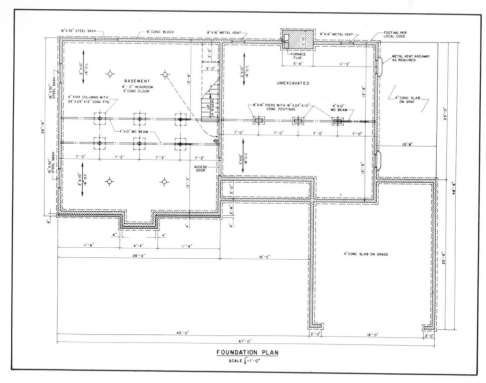

Fig. 1-1 Typical working drawing

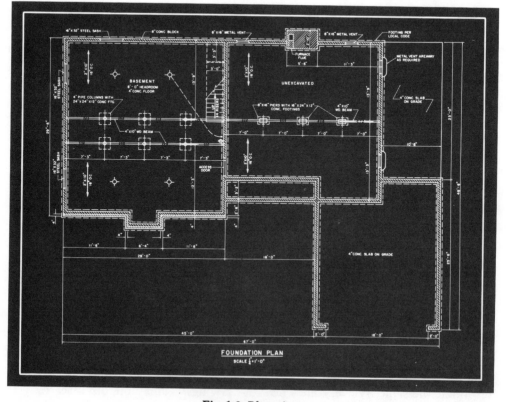

Fig. 1-2 Blueprint

Blueprinting

The original drawing is done on translucent (nearly transparent) paper *(vellum)* or plastic film. The original is held against a sheet of light-sensitive paper in a glass frame. The two sheets are exposed to a bright light for a specified time period. The light strikes the light-sensitive sheet everywhere except where lines are drawn on the original. Wherever there are marks on the original, no light strikes the sensitized surface.

After exposure, the sensitized paper is washed with water. Where the sensitized coating has been exposed to light, it hardens and turns blue in washing. Where the coating was shielded from the light, it remains soft and is washed away by the water. This leaves a blue background with white lines, figure 1-2. The blueprint is then washed with a chemical fixing agent to prevent the print from further developing. As a final step, the fixing agent is washed off and the blueprint is hung to dry.

For many years the blueprint process was used for almost all drawing reproduction. Although other processes have largely replaced blueprinting, it is still common to refer to all reproductions of drawings as blueprints.

Diazo Process

A more widely used method of reproduction uses ammonia vapor as a developing agent. This is the *diazo process*. In this process, the sensitized paper and the original drawing are exposed to a strong light, as in the blueprint process. After exposure, the sensitized paper is exposed to ammonia vapor. No fixing or washing is necessary. The finished print is free from the distortion usually caused by the washing and drying operations, figure 1-3.

A print made by the diazo process is the reverse of a blueprint. The background is white and the lines are blue.

Photo-Reproduction Printing

Recently, to fill the need for more efficient ways to produce large quantities of quality prints, a photographic method has been used. The original is photographed on a large copy camera. Then the negative is developed as in regular photography. Instead of printing the negative on photographic paper, it is printed on an offset printing plate. This plate is attached to an offset printing press. Offset printing is widely used for books, magazines, and newspapers. A single offset plate can be used to print several hundred copies in less than one hour, if necessary. Another advantage of the photographic

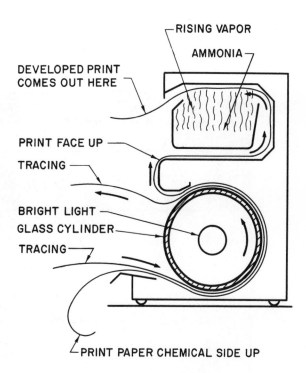

ROLLERS MOVE THE TRACING AND PRINT
AROUND THE LIGHT AND MOVE THE PRINT
PAST THE RISING AMMONIA VAPOR

Fig. 1-3 The Diazo Process

process is that it allows easy reductions in size, thereby reducing mailing and storage costs.

Both the photo-reproduction and diazo process result in white prints (white background with colored lines). Because blueprints were once so widely used, white prints are often called blueprints. It is not correct, however, to refer to all drawings as plans. A plan is a specific type of drawing which will be discussed later.

ASSIGNMENT

Questions

1. What is the main purpose of construction drawings? _____
    _____

2. What three basic characteristics of a building are shown on drawings?
    _____

3. Why is it important for construction drawings to be made according
    to established rules? _____

4. In order to make blueprints or diazo prints, the original must be on a
    _____ sheet.

5. What is a blueprint? _____

6. How is a diazo print different from a blueprint? _____
    _____

7. Briefly describe the diazo process. _____
    _____

8. What process is best suited for reducing the size of prints? _____
    _____

9. What is done with the original drawings after all prints are made?
    _____

10. What is a whiteprint? _____

UNIT 2 ORTHOGRAPHIC PROJECTIONS

OBJECTIVES

After completing this unit, the student will be able to:

- visualize the actual shape of an object shown in orthographic projection.

- identify the location of the various views in orthographic projection.

There are basically two ways to draw a three-dimensional object on a flat sheet of paper. In *pictorial drawings* the object is drawn like it actually looks. These types of drawings show several sides of an object in one view. This tends to crowd information. Furthermore, to make the drawing look like the object, many angles must be distorted and some lines must be shortened. To communicate information more accurately, working drawings usually use orthographic projection.

In *orthographic projection* two or more views of the object are drawn. Each view shows only one side of the object. The views are always positioned in the same place on the drawing, so the person reading the drawing knows where to find them.

To illustrate the position of the views, assume that the stepped block in figure 2-1 is suspended inside a hinged glass box, figure 2-2.

Looking in the direction of arrow ①, the rectangular outline of the front is shown. The line across the rectangle is the top of the step. In this view the length, overall height, and height of the step can be seen. Draw this view on the front surface of the box.

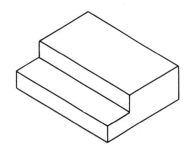

Fig. 2-1 Stepped block

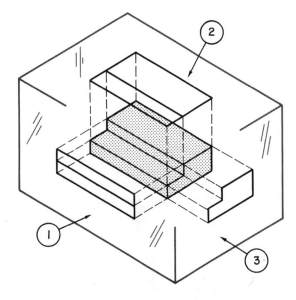

Fig. 2-2 Stepped block suspended inside glass box

5

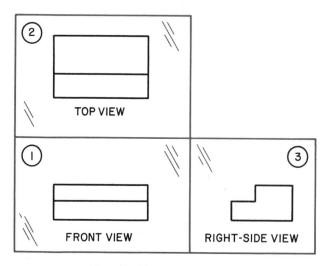

Fig. 2-3 Glass box unfolded

Looking in the direction of arrow ②, the rectangular outline of the top is shown. The line across this rectangle is the back of the step. In this view the length, overall depth, and the depth of the step can be seen. Draw this view on the top surface of the box.

Looking in the direction of arrow ③, the end of the step is shown. In this view the overall height, height of the step, overall depth, and depth of the step can be seen. Drawing this view on the end of the box provides enough views to illustrate a typical drawing.

What has been done up to this point is to project the views of the block away from the block itself, onto the glass. The three views are still in three separate planes. Since a sheet of drawing paper is all in one plane, the next step is to unfold the three planes of the box so they form one plane. The positions of the three views on the flattened-out glass box are shown in figure 2-3. The picture shows the correct relationship of these views on a working drawing or an orthographic projection.

Note the relationship of each of these views to each other. View ② is located directly above and in line with View ①. Both views have a common length. View ③ is located to the right side of and directly in line with View ①. Both of these views share common dimensions, the overall height, and the height of the step.

If it is necessary to show an object in other views, the process is the same. The rear view is projected onto the back of the glass box. The left-end view is projected onto the left end of the box. Working drawings produced for the building trades include enough views to show all necessary information. However, it is not considered a good practice to repeat information unnecessarily. Round objects, for example, often require only two views. An additional orthographic view of the plug shown in figure 2-4 would not provide more information.

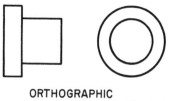

ORTHOGRAPHIC

PICTORIAL

Fig. 2-4 Plug

ASSIGNMENT

A.   Questions

1. Name 2 views in orthographic projection that show the overall length of an object. _____

2. Name 2 views in orthographic projection that show the overall height of an object. _____

3. The correct relationship of the various views on a working drawing is important so _____ .

For questions 4-8, refer to the drawing of the corner bracket.

4. Which line or surface in the top view represents (C) ?   _____

5. Which line or surface in the right-side view represents (A) ?   _____

6. Which line or surface in the front view represents (H) ?   _____

7. Which line or surface in the right-side view represents (H) ?   _____

8. Which line or surface in the top view represents (I) ?   _____

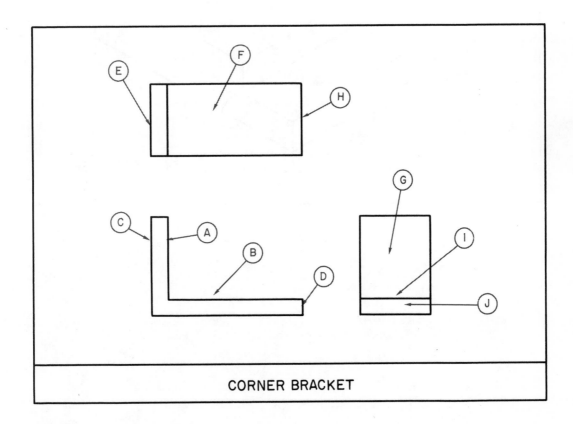

CORNER BRACKET

B.   Sketching

Step 1   Make a three-view drawing of the concrete steps.

Step 2   Let each square of the drawing sheet represent 3".

Step 3   Omit all dimensions.

Step 4   Clearly print the name of each view.

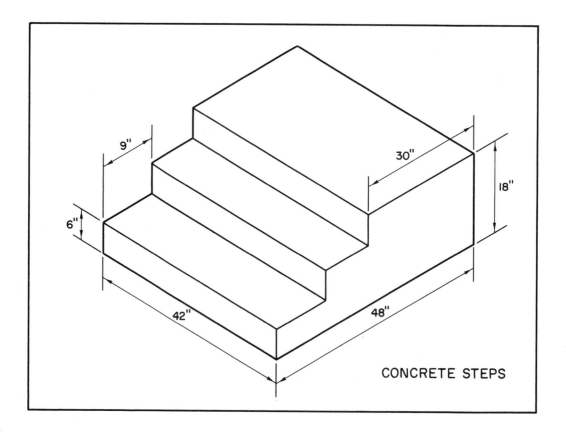

CONCRETE STEPS

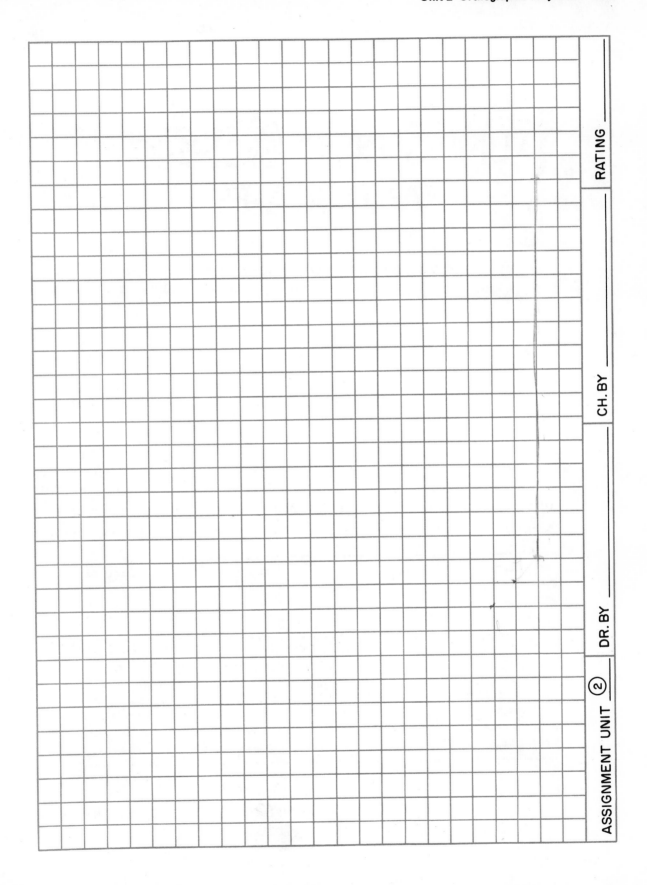

ASSIGNMENT UNIT ②   DR. BY   CH. BY   RATING

UNIT 3 DIMENSIONING AND SCALES

OBJECTIVES

After completing this unit, the student will be able to:

- identify dimensions on a drawing.
- read an architect's scale.

DIMENSIONING

Dimensions are included on a drawing to show the size and location of all parts. The methods of showing the necessary dimensions are standardized to insure uniform interpretation. The sketch of the wall in figure 3-1 shows an accepted form of dimensioning.

The *extension lines* that show what is dimensioned are a continuation of the lines of the object itself. To avoid confusion between the object lines and the extension lines, a short break occurs between them. For further distinction, the object lines are drawn fairly thick, while the extension lines are drawn thin but sharp enough to be distinct.

The *dimension line* is drawn at right angles to the extension lines. It extends from one extension line to the other. The weight of this line is the same as that of the extension line — thin, but sharp and distinct. The arrowheads

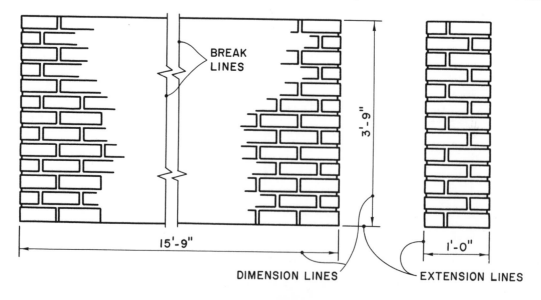

Fig. 3-1 Extension and dimension lines in use

at each end of this line are used to clearly show the beginning and ending points of the dimension. These arrowheads are all drawn to a uniform size and are usually made about three times as long as they are wide. Some drawings are dimensioned using slashes or ticks at the ends of the dimension lines, figure 3-2.

When long objects must be shown in a small space, *break lines* are used, figure 3-1. Break lines indicate that the entire length has not been drawn. Dimension lines are not broken when break lines are used.

Dimensions are given in feet and inches, for example, 6'-8" or 1'-3". Even those dimensions that are an even number of feet are dimensioned in this manner. Typical dimensions of this type are 6'-0", 2'-0", and 12'-0". This is done to eliminate the possibility of error through misinterpretation of a dimension. Exceptions to this rule are those dimensions that are standards of construction, such as the center-to-center distance of studs, joists, or rafters. This distance is given in inches as in 24" OC (On Center), 16" OC, or 16" CC (Center to Center). On some drawings where most dimensions are less than one foot, the inch marks are left off.

Dimensioning in Small Spaces

In many instances, the space between the two extension lines is too small to permit drawing a dimension line with two arrowheads and a printed dimension. Figure 3-3 shows the accepted methods of dimensioning under such conditions. In all cases, the dimensions are placed outside the object lines rather than within the drawing.

Dimensioning Structural Members

On any set of drawings, dimensions serve two important functions: to indicate the location of a specific construction feature and to indicate size. In architectural drawing,

extension and dimension lines are used to show overall building sizes and locate building features.

The structural parts themselves are usually dimensioned for size. A line with an arrowhead that leads from a clear space where dimensions or notes are written to the structural member is called a *leader*. Figure 3-4, page 12, shows a typical example of this form of dimensioning.

Because of the greatly reduced size of the drawing, most structural members appear very small and would be extremely difficult to dimension if extension and dimension lines were used in the standard manner.

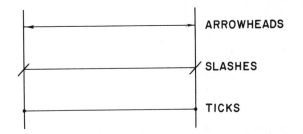

Fig. 3-2 Three forms of dimensioning

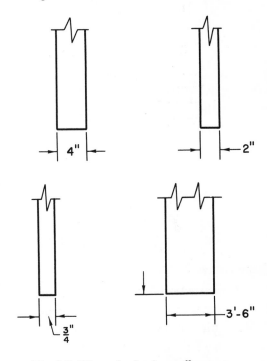

Fig. 3-3 Dimensioning in small spaces

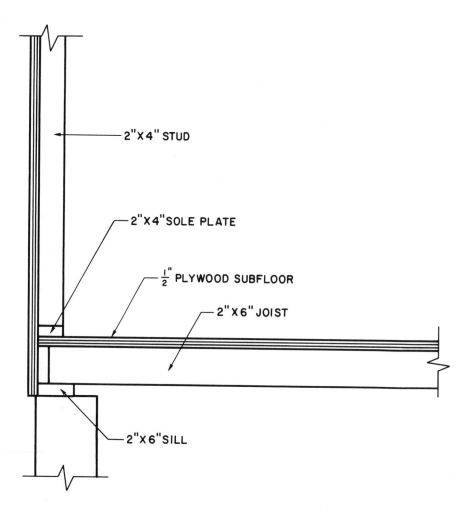

Fig. 3-4 Leaders used on a drawing

Also, moving the dimension to a clear space permits the architect to include other important information. In figure 3-4, the dimension for each structural part includes the name and purpose of the part. Note, for example, the dimension 1/2" plywood subfloor. In addition to the size, this dimension contains a description of the kind of material used and its purpose in the construction.

Scale Drawings

Construction work is usually too large to be drawn actual size on a drawing sheet. This requires drawing everything proportionately smaller. Although all dimensions should be clearly indicated on the blueprints, it is sometimes necessary to measure the scale drawings to determine a dimension. The tool used to measure these scale drawings is the *architect's scale.*

Reading an Architect's Scale

The architect's scale is *open divided,* figure 3-5. This means the scales have the main units undivided, and a fully subdivided, extra unit placed at the zero end of the scales.

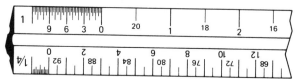

Fig. 3-5 Architect's triangular scale

Listed below are eleven scales found on the architect's triangular scale:

Full scale

3/32″ = 1′- 0″
1/8″ = 1′- 0″
3/16″ = 1′- 0″
1/4″ = 1′- 0″
3/8″ = 1′- 0″
1/2″ = 1′- 0″
3/4″ = 1′- 0″
1″ = 1′- 0″
1 1/2″= 1′- 0″
3″ = 1′- 0″

Two scales are combined on each face, except the full-size scale which is fully divided into sixteenths. The combined scales work together because one is twice as large as the other, and their zero points and extra divided units are on opposite ends of the scale.

Architectural drawings use feet and inches as the major units of measurement. The architect's scale is broken down into these units in reduced scales. This is done so that large buildings and details can be drawn on paper. This makes the drawings smaller and easier to handle.

The fraction, or number, near the zero at each end of the scale indicates the unit length in inches that is used on the drawing to represent one foot of the actual building. The extra unit near the zero end of the scale is subdivided into twelfths of a foot, or inches, as well as fractions of inches on the larger scales.

Most house plans and small buildings are drawn to the 1/4-inch scale. This means that each quarter of an inch on the drawing equals one foot of the actual size of the

building. For example, a line drawn 3 inches long represents 12 feet on the building. The scale of the drawing is noted on the drawing and is usually given in the title box on each drawing. Sometimes when special details are given, the scale is placed directly under the detail.

To read the architect's triangular scale, turn it to the 1/4-inch scale. The scale is divided on the left from the zero towards the 1/4 mark so that each line represents one inch. Counting the marks from the zero toward the 1/4 mark, there are twelve lines marked on the scale. Each one of these lines is one inch on the 1/4″ = 1′-0″ scale.

The fraction 1/8 is on the opposite end of the same scale, figure 3-6. This is the 1/8-inch scale and is read from the right to the left. Notice that the divided unit is only half as large as the one on the 1/4-inch end of the scale. Counting the lines from zero toward the 1/8 mark, there are only six lines. This means that each line represents two inches at the 1/8-inch scale.

Now look at the 1 1/2-inch scale, figure 3-7. The divided unit is broken into twelfths of an inch and also a fractional part of an inch. Reading from the zero toward the number 1 1/2, notice the figures 3, 6, and 9. These figures represent the measurements of 3 inches, 6 inches, and 9 inches at the 1 1/2″ = 1′-0″ scale. From the zero to the first long mark that represents one inch (which is the same length as the mark shown at 3) are 4 lines. This means that each line on the scale is equal to 1/4 of an inch. Reading the zero to the 3, read each line as follows: 1/4, 1/2, 3/4, 1, 1 1/4, 1 1/2, 1 3/4, 2, 2 1/4, 2 1/2, 2 3/4, and 3 inches.

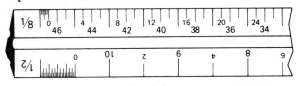

Fig. 3-6

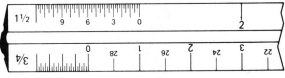

Fig. 3-7

ASSIGNMENT

A.   Reading Scales

1. _____

2. _____

3. _____

4. _____

5. _____

6. _____

7. _____

8. _____

9. _____

10. _____

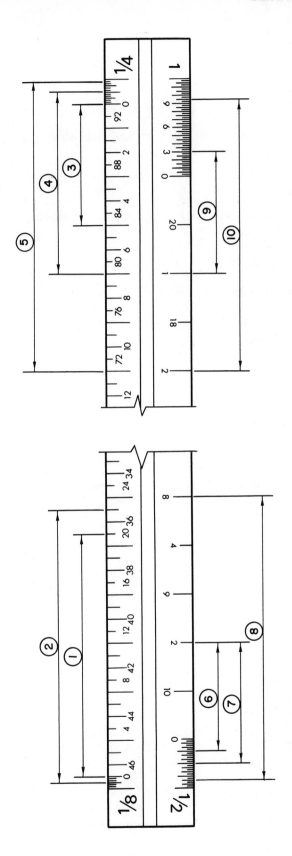

B.   Sketching

Step 1   Make a three-view working drawing of the concrete foundation complete with dimensions.

Step 2   Let each square of the drawing sheet represent 12″.

Step 3   Indicate a break line in the front and right-side views.

C.   Questions

1.   What is the overall height of the foundation including the footing?   _____

2.   What is the width of the footing?   _____

3.   How thick is the concrete wall?   _____

4.   How much does the footing project beyond each face of the foundation wall?   _____

5.   What is the difference in length of the two walls which form the corner?   _____

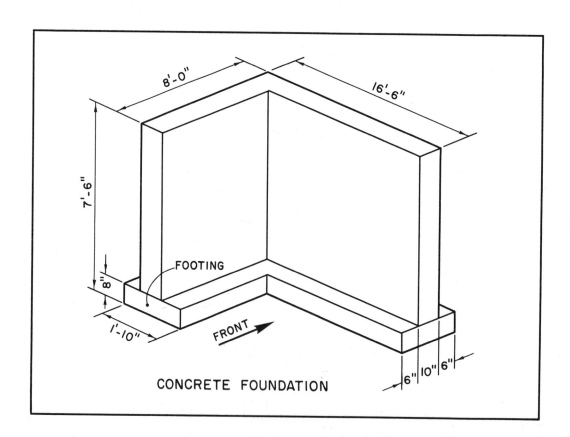

CONCRETE FOUNDATION

ASSIGNMENT UNIT ③   DR. BY ———   CH. BY ———   RATING ———

UNIT 4 HIDDEN EDGES

OBJECTIVES

After completing this unit, the student will be able to:

- explain the importance of showing hidden edges on a working drawing.
- indicate a hidden edge on a working drawing.

HIDDEN LINES

In construction work many of the important surfaces and edges are hidden from view. Since these surfaces and edges are important if the instructions are to be complete, it is necessary to show them in the working drawing. To avoid confusion with the visible surfaces and edges which are shown by object lines, the hidden edges are represented by a line of dashes, figure 4-1.

This line of dashes is drawn slightly thinner than the object lines so that it does not detract from the basic shape of the outline. It is still drawn considerably heavier than the extension and dimension lines. Care should be taken to make the dashes a uniform length. There should also be an approximately uniform space between dashes. Otherwise, this type of line will be confused with broken lines used for other purposes.

The concrete block shown in figure 4-1 is an excellent example of how a hidden line is used on a working drawing. If the front view were drawn as we see it, the rectangular holes would not be shown. The result of eliminating the hidden lines would be to leave the depth of the holes to the imagination. The addition of the hidden lines to the front view shows the depth of the holes clearly.

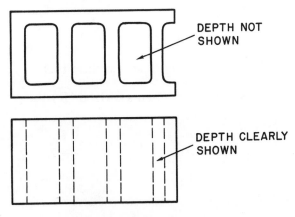

DEPTH NOT
SHOWN

DEPTH CLEARLY
SHOWN

Fig. 4-1 Hidden lines

DIMENSIONING HIDDEN EDGES

Care should be taken when dimensioning a drawing that contains hidden lines. Wherever possible, the dimensions should be shown on the view that contains the visible edge lines. This practice is followed because it is easier to interpret. Figure 4-2 illustrates the preferred practice.

All hidden edges and surfaces which are important to understand the drawing should be shown. In some instances there are so many hidden lines that the drawing becomes confusing. To simplify the drawing, the accepted practice is to show the view with a minimum of hidden lines. A detail drawing is added to clarify the actual construction features.

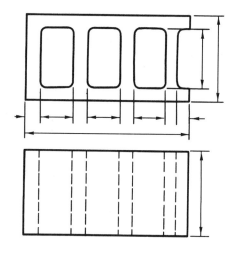

Fig. 4-2 Preferred dimensioning

ASSIGNMENT

A. Blueprint Reading. Refer to the drawing of the cabinet.

1. What line in the side view represents (A) ? _____

2. What line in the front view represents (B) ? _____

3. What line in the side view represents (C) ? _____

4. What line in the side view represents (E) ? _____

5. What is dimension (H) ? _____

6. What is the thickness of the part indicated by (I) ? _____

7. What line in the front view represents (D) ? _____

8. What is dimension (J) ? _____

9. What line in the front view represents (F) ? _____

10. What line in the front view represents surface (R) ? _____

11. What line in the side view represents surface (R) ? _____

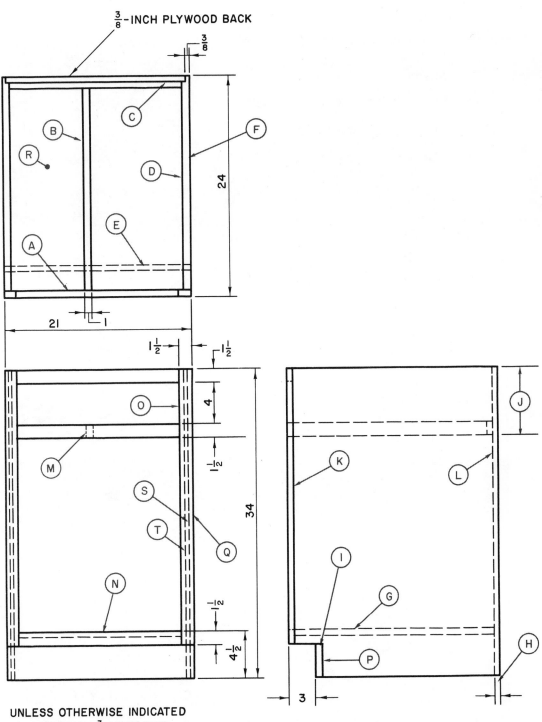

$\frac{3}{8}$-INCH PLYWOOD BACK

$\frac{3}{8}$

C

B

R

F

D

24

E

A

21

1

$1\frac{1}{2}$ $1\frac{1}{2}$

O

4

J

M

$\frac{1}{2}$

K

L

S

34

T

Q

I

N

G

$\frac{1}{2}$

P

H

$4\frac{1}{2}$

3

UNLESS OTHERWISE INDICATED
ALL MATERIAL $\frac{3}{4}$-INCH PINE

CABINET

B.   Sketching

Step 1 Make a two-view working drawing of the hollow keystone complete with dimensions.

Step 2 Make the drawing to a scale of 3″ = 1′-0″.

C.   Questions

1. What is the length of the keystone?   _____

2. What is the width at the top?   _____

3. What is the width at the bottom?   _____

4. Will the front view be affected if the center web is moved up?   _____

5. Is the center web the same thickness as the walls of the keystone?   _____

6. What do the dash lines of the front view represent?   _____

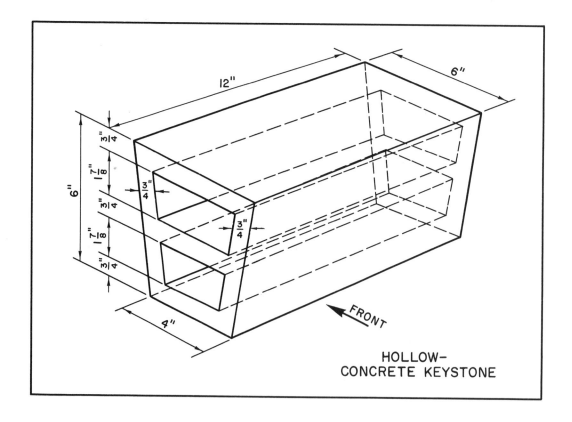

HOLLOW-
CONCRETE KEYSTONE

ASSIGNMENT UNIT ④   DR. BY   CH. BY   RATING

UNIT 5 CIRCLES AND ARCS

OBJECTIVES

After completing this unit, the student will be able to:

- show how circles and arcs are drawn.
- use standard dimensioning practice for circles and arcs.

CIRCLES

The first step in drawing a circle is to locate its center. When the center has been located, the circle is drawn with a compass. To do this, the compass is set to the *radius* (one-half the diameter). The point of the compass is then set at the center mark, and the compass is pivoted around this point to draw the circle.

On a drawing, the center of a circle is indicated by the intersection of two centerlines. These lines are used solely for the accurate location and construction of the circle. While these centerlines are important to understand the drawing, they must not be confused with the visible or hidden lines. A centerline is a thin, sharp line about the same weight as extension and dimension lines, figure 5-1. It is made up of long dashes broken with single short dashes.

Circular objects can usually be shown completely in two views; the front and the side. A top view would be a duplication of the side and is, therefore, unnecessary. In order that centerlines are not confused as part of the object, they are normally drawn beyond the object lines.

DIMENSIONING A CIRCLE

Centerlines are also used to dimension the location of the center of a circle, figure 5-2, page 26.

The circles themselves are dimensioned as shown in figure 5-3, A through D, page 26. Method A is used when there is not enough

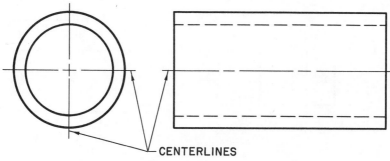

CENTERLINES

Fig. 5-1 Centerlines

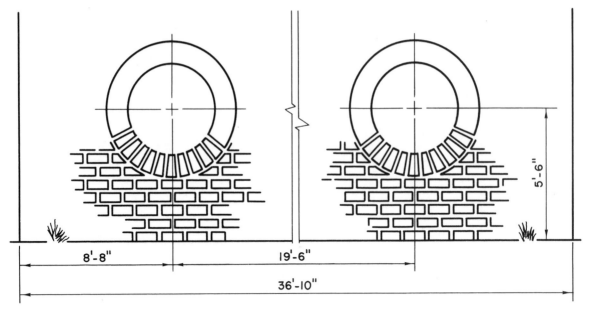

Fig. 5-2 Dimensioning circles

room to crowd the dimension line, arrows, dimensions, and centerlines within the circle. Method B is used for dimensioning large circles. The dimension line is drawn at an angle to avoid overlapping a centerline. Note that the diameter of the circle — not the radius — is always used for dimensioning purposes. Method C is used to dimension cylinders. As shown by Method D, when several circles are shown, they are usually located by dimensions that are given from the center of one circle to the center of the next.

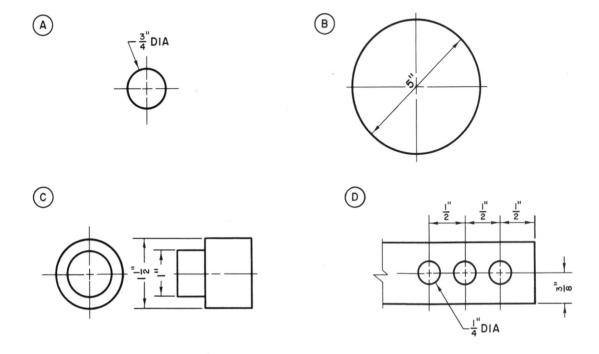

Fig. 5-3 Methods of dimensioning circles

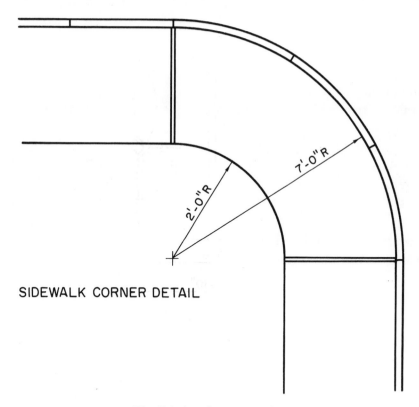

Fig. 5-4 Arcs in construction

DRAWING AND DIMENSIONING ARCS

An *arc* is a part of a circle or an incomplete circle. Figure 5-4 shows a typical application of arcs in sidewalk construction.

Like circles, arcs are located by their center points. Dimensions are given from this point for both the location and the size of the arc. The major difference is that the arc dimension is given as a radius, and the circle dimension is given as a diameter.

The accepted methods of dimensioning the size of an arc are shown in figure 5-5. The dimension line is run at an angle from the intersection of the centerlines to the arc. Only one arrow is used, touching the object line or arc.

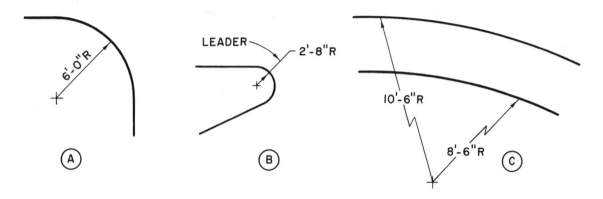

Fig. 5-5 Dimensioning arcs

On the small radius arc at B, a leader is used for the dimension. Although the dimension itself is printed outside of the object, only one arrow is used.

To dimension an arc with a very large radius, as shown at C, frequently requires that the dimension line be run through other parts of the drawing. To avoid possible confusion, the dimension line is started at the intersection of the centerlines, discontinued where it passes through the other details, and started again near the arc. Many drafters and architects use a zigzag in the dimension line to indicate that it has been broken along its length.

BREAK LINES

The methods of showing break lines in cylindrical and rectangular objects vary as shown in figure 5-6.

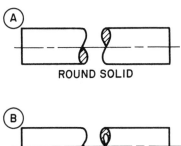
ROUND SOLID

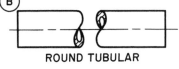
ROUND TUBULAR

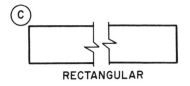
RECTANGULAR

Fig. 5-6 Break lines

ASSIGNMENT

A.   Blueprint Reading. Refer to the drawing of the lockset mortise.

1. Which lines in the right-side view represent hole (A) ?   _____

2. Which lines in the front (left-side) view represent hole (B) ?   _____

3. What is dimension (C) ?   _____

4. Which surface in the right-side view represents (F) ?   _____

5. Which surface in the right-side view represents (M) ?   _____

6. What is dimension (N) ?   _____

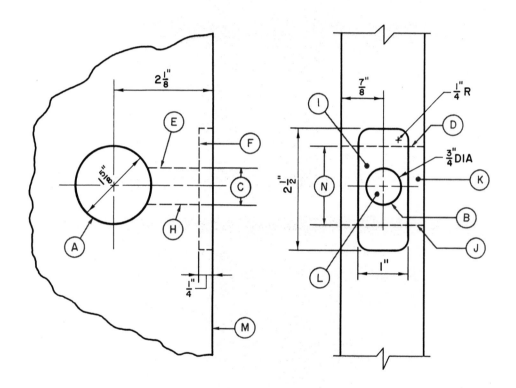

LOCKSET MORTISE

B. Sketching

Step 1 Make a two-view drawing of the drain pipe complete with dimensions.

Step 2 Make the drawing to a scale of 3″ = 1′-0″.

Step 3 Show a break line in the right-side view.

C. Questions

1. What is the overall length of the pipe? _____

2. Give the outside diameter and the inside diameter of the large end of the drain pipe. _____

3. What effect does a change in length have on the front view? _____

4. Is the wall thickness of the pipe the same for its entire length? What is the wall thickness? _____

5. Which views are affected if the 7″ dimension is increased? _____

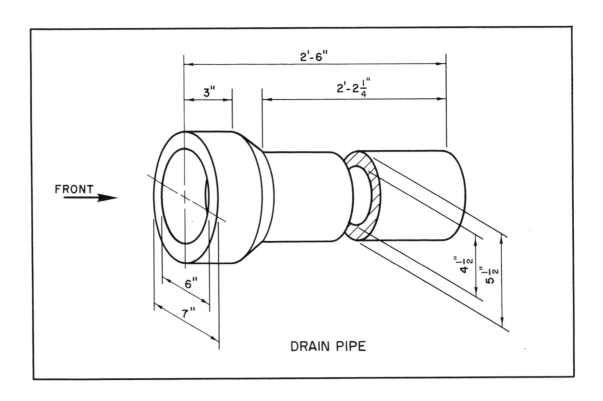

DRAIN PIPE

ASSIGNMENT UNIT ⑤   DR. BY ____   CH. BY ____   RATING ____

UNIT 6 PLANS, ELEVATIONS, AND SECTIONS

OBJECTIVES

After completing this unit, the student will be able to:

- read simple plan views, elevation views, and section views.

- determine the relationship between the various views of a set of working drawings.

PLANS

Working drawings for construction are almost always done by orthographic projection. However, to help identify the views, they are given names. The top view is called a *plan* or *plan view,* figure 6-1. In order to show as much information as possible, plan views are drawn at several points in a building. A typical set of working drawings includes a basement plan, floor plan, and plot plan.

Where it is necessary to show interior detail, such as on a floor plan, an imaginary cut is made through the building, figure 6-2. For a floor plan, this cut is made at a height that passes through the windows, doors, and other wall openings. Looking straight down at this imaginary cut, one sees the floor plan, figure 6-3. This shows the arrangement of rooms, locations of doors and windows, and other important information. To further

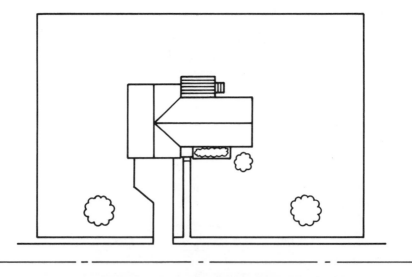

Fig. 6-1 A plot plan is a common type of plan view.

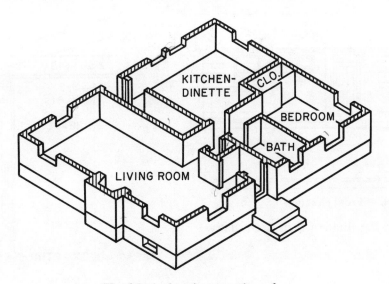

Fig. 6-2 An imaginary cut is made.

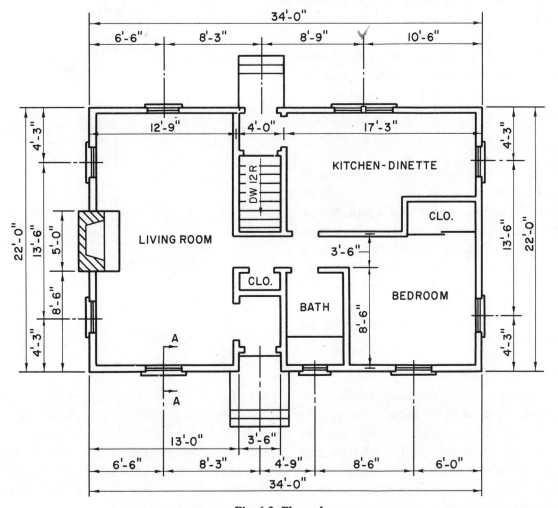

Fig. 6-3 Floor plan

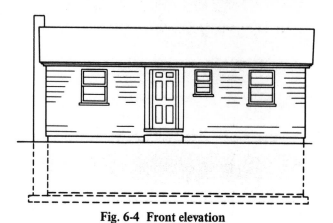

Fig. 6-4 Front elevation

simplify the drawing, hidden lines are usually omitted.

ELEVATIONS

Drawings which show height, such as front views and side views, are called *elevations*. Elevation drawings are named according to their location. A typical set of working drawings includes elevations of each side of the building. Elevations do not show interior detail, figure 6-4.

SECTIONS

It is not possible to show all of the necessary information in the plans and elevations. To see the structural parts of a wall, for example, it is necessary to draw a section view, figure 6-5. This is the result of an imaginary cut through the building, similar to that made for the floor plan. Most section views are vertical, but horizontal (or plan) sections may be included. In section views the parts are usually labeled.

REFERENCE LINES

To locate clearly the position where the structure is cut away to show a section, the architect uses a *reference line* or *cutting-plane line* through the structure. The reference line has an arrow on each end showing the direction in which the architect views the structure to obtain the sectional view.

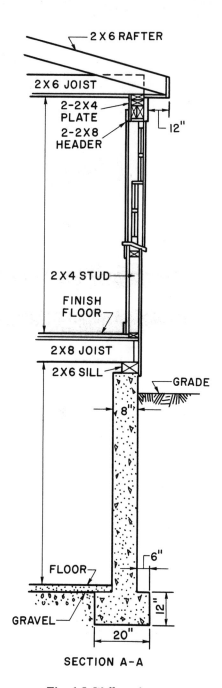

Fig. 6-5 Wall section

In a drawing that contains many reference lines, the line is identified with letters at each end, such as A-A, B-B, C-C. A typical set of plans may contain many sections, each identified with the same letters as its corresponding reference line, such as section A-A, section B-B, and section C-C, figure 6-3.

ASSIGNMENT

A. Questions

1. Which view shows what a person in the illustration would see?

a. Plan view
b. Right elevation
c. Left elevation
d. Section view

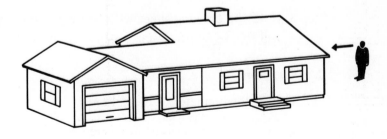

2. Which view shows the location of the kitchen?

a. Floor plan
b. Wall section
c. Front elevation
d. Side elevation

3. Which view shows the size of the materials used in the walls?

a. Floor plan
b. Wall section
c. Any elevation
d. Basement plan

4. What is indicated by a heavy line through part of a drawing with an arrowhead and the letter B at each end?

a. A missing dimension
b. A window or door
c. A floor plan
d. A section view

5. Which view in a set of construction drawings corresponds with the top view in orthographic projection?

a. Plan
b. Front elevation
c. Right-side elevation
d. Section

6. Which view in a set of construction drawings corresponds with the front view in orthographic projection?

a. Plan
b. Front elevation
c. Right-side elevation
d. Section

B.   Sketching

Step 1 Draw a plan view and section view of the pipe column. The section view is in place of the front elevation.

Step 2 Make the drawing to a scale of 1 1/2″ = 1′-0″.

Step 3 Hold the drawing sheet with its long side vertical so that the drawing will fit. Use a break line for the top of the column.

C.   Questions

1. What is the diameter of the column? _____

2. What are the dimensions of the steel base? _____

3. What are the dimensions of the footing? _____

4. Is a third view necessary? Why or why not? _____

5. Will the plan view be affected if the height of the footing is increased or decreased? _____

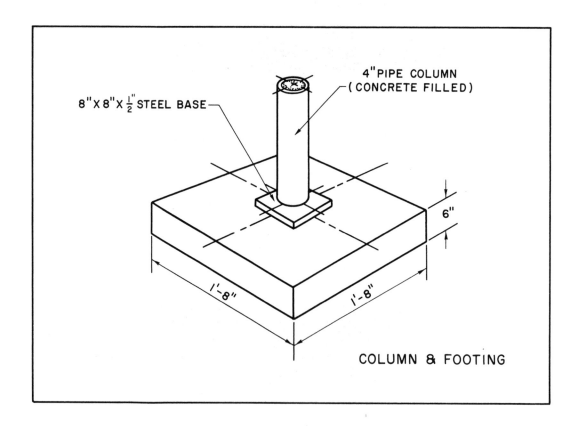

8″X 8″X $\frac{1}{2}$″ STEEL BASE

4″ PIPE COLUMN (CONCRETE FILLED)

6″

1′-8″   1′-8″

COLUMN & FOOTING

RATING

CH. BY

DR. BY

ASSIGNMENT UNIT ⑥

UNIT 7 SYMBOLS, ABBREVIATIONS, AND NOTES

OBJECTIVES

After completing this unit, the student will be able to:

- interpret common symbols found on drawings.
- explain the importance of notes on drawings.
- interpret common abbreviations.

SYMBOLS

In order for the architect, engineer, or drafter to make drawings useful, there must be a way to illustrate materials. The simple outline of an object shows its shape. It does not indicate whether it is made of steel, concrete, or wood.

To show materials, the drafter uses symbols. There are two generally accepted

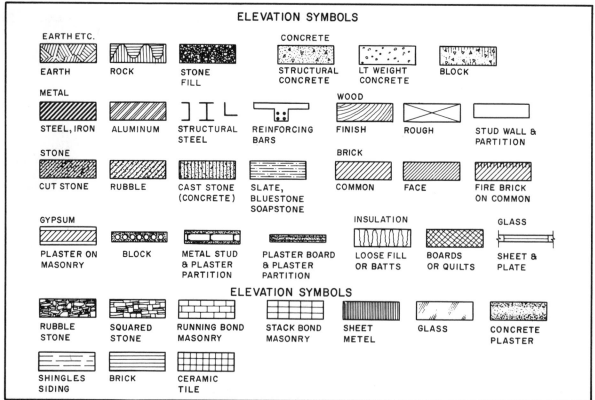

Fig. 7-1 Symbols found on architectural drawings

sets of material symbols. One set is used on plan and section views. The other set is used on elevations. Figure 7-1 shows the most common material symbols.

In addition to showing materials, symbols are used to show objects that would require too much detail if drawn in a conventional way. These objects include plumbing fixtures, electrical fixtures, and some mechanical devices, figure 7-2.

ABBREVIATIONS

Many words or phrases are standard in the construction language. To eliminate the need for writing these out every time they are used, standard abbreviations are used, figure 7-3, page 40.

NOTES

Although drawings are used to illustrate graphically how a structure is to be built, not all information can be shown with lines, symbols, and dimensions. Notes are added to drawings to explain items that cannot be readily drawn. Notes are not used, however, to replace complete and detailed drawings. Notes should be easily understood by all who will read the drawings. Notice that in figure 7-4, page 41, the notes are easy to understand without prior knowledge of the building.

General notes, those which apply to many parts of the structure, are neatly lettered in an open area of the drawing. Notes that explain a specific part of the construction are keyed to that point with a leader.

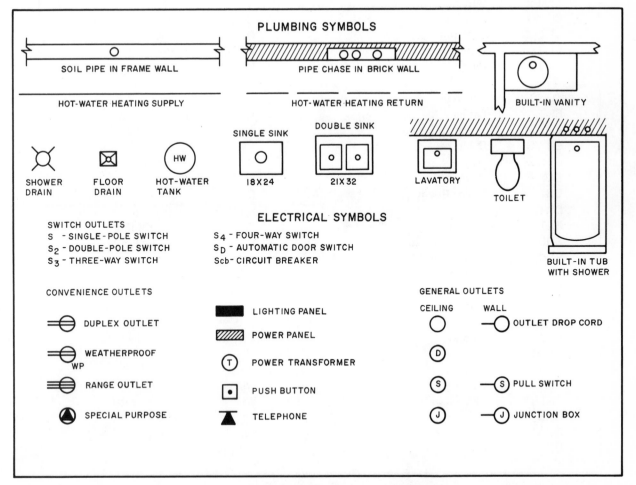

Fig. 7-2 Mechanical and electrical symbols

AWG	American Wire Gage	GYP	Gypsum
AMP or A	Ampere	HB	Hose Bibb
APVD	Approved	HD	Head
ASPH	Asphalt	HDWD	Hardwood
ASSY	Assembly	HW	Hot Water
B	Bathroom	ID	Inside Diameter
BD	Board	INSUL	Insulation
BL	Building	INTR	Interior
BLK	Block	KD	Kiln Dried
BLT	Bolt	KIT	Kitchen
BM	Beam, Bench Mark, or Board Measure	LBR	Lumber
BOT	Bottom	LG	Length
BR	Bedroom	LNTL	Lintel
BRK	Brick	MATL	Material
BSMT	Basement	MFR	Manufacturer
BTU	British Thermal Unit	MLDG	Molding
CB	Circuit Breaker	MSNRY	Masonry
CCB	Concrete Block	NOM	Nominal
CFM	Cubic Feet Per Minute	OC	On Center
CI	Cast Iron	OD	Outside Diameter
CL or ₵	Centerline	PC	Piece
CLG	Ceiling	PLMB	Plumbing
CLO	Closet	PLY WD	Plywood
COL	Column	PN	Part Number
CONC	Concrete	PNT	Paint
CSG	Casing	R	Radius
C to C	Center to Center	REINF	Reinforced
CU YD	Cubic Yard	RM	Room
DBL	Double	RTN	Return
DIA	Diameter	SDG	Siding
DR	Dining Room	SEW	Sewer
DWL	Dowel	SHTHG	Sheathing
ENTR	Entrance	SPEC	Specification
EQL SP	Equally Spaced	SQ FT	Square Foot
EXC	Excavate or Except	STD	Standard
EXT	Exterior or Extinguisher	SURF	Surface
FD	Floor Drain	SUSP	Suspend
FDN	Foundation	T & G	Tongue and Groove
FL	Floor	THK	Thick
FLG	Flooring	UNFIN	Unfinished
FNSH	Finish	V	Volt
FTG	Fitting or Footing	W	Watt
GA	Gage	WD	Wood
GALVI	Galvanized Iron	WH	Water Heater
GAR	Garage	WI	Wrought Iron
GL	Glass	YD	Yard
GR	Grade		

Fig. 7-3 Commonly used abbreviations

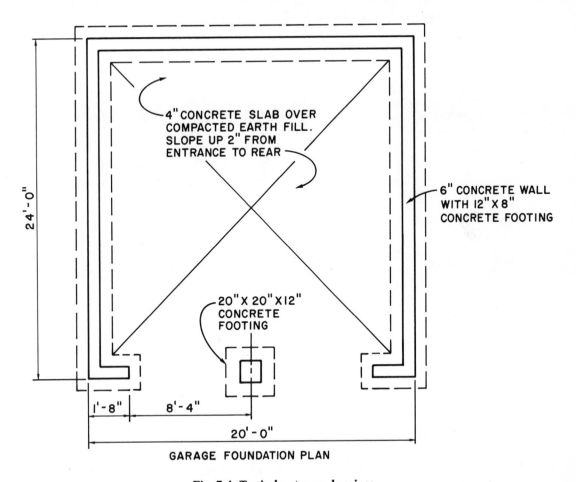

GARAGE FOUNDATION PLAN

Fig. 7-4 Typical notes on drawings

ASSIGNMENT

A.   Questions

Write the abbreviation for each of the following:

1. Building   _____

2. Concrete   _____

3. Plywood   _____

4. Exterior   _____

5. Interior   _____

6. On center   _____

7. Foundation   _____

8. Wood   _____

9. Insulation   _____

10. Cubic yards   _____

B. **Identification. Refer to the drawings of the fireplace.**

What material is indicated by each of the following:

A   _____   F   _____

B   _____   G   _____

C   _____   H   _____

D   _____   I   _____

E   _____   J   _____

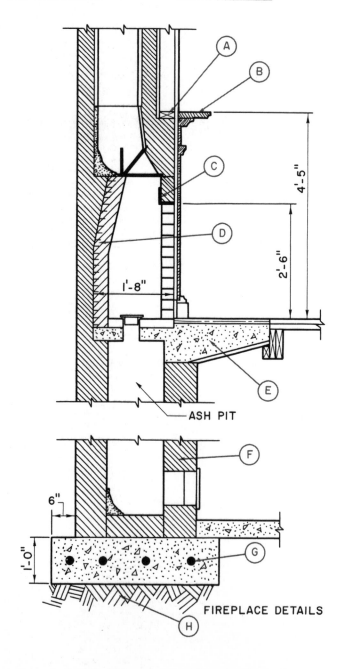

FIREPLACE DETAILS

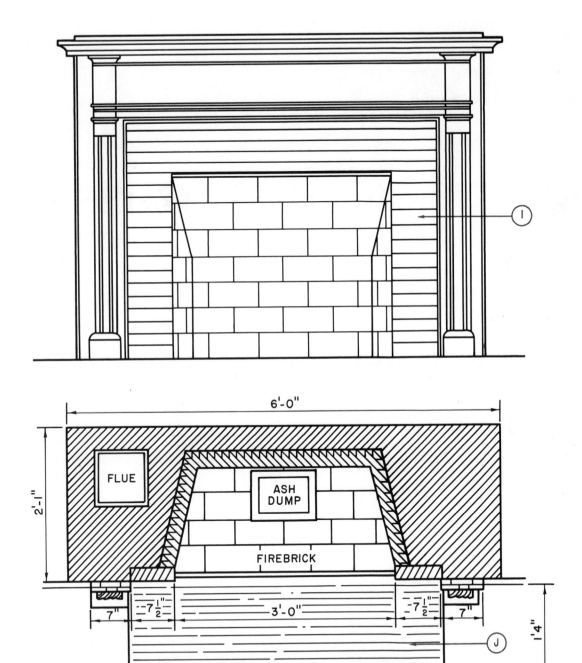

Section 2 TRADE SKETCHING

UNIT 8 SKETCHING STRAIGHT LINES

OBJECTIVES

After completing this unit, the student will be able to:

- sketch straight lines.
- explain proportion in sketching.

IMPORTANCE OF SKETCHING

The old saying "a picture is worth a thousand words," is particularly true to construction workers. To them a drawing is a set of instructions. They read drawings as others would read a manual of instructions. The engineer, architect, or foreman uses a pencil sketch to illustrate an idea.

A worker on the job who thinks of a time-saving device or a new method of construction uses a sketch to explain the idea to others. In many cases, a pencil sketch that has been suitably initialed is used as authority to proceed with a job. Even the language barrier offers no handicap to the foreman who has a pencil and paper handy.

The pencil sketch plays an important part in the building trades. Any worker in these trades who wants to become a foreman or superintendent should be able to draw neat sketches.

Since this type of sketching is mechanical in nature, the trainee does not need any artistic talent, although such talent is not a drawback. The prerequisites to this form of expression are neatness in work habits, attention to detail, and the ability to visualize. Perhaps the most important of these characteristics is the ability to visualize.

Sketches are used in many cases in preference to an instrument drawing because they can be made so quickly and do not require any tools other than paper, pencil, and eraser. In order to be useful, however, the sketch should be carefully and neatly drawn. The lines should be clean and straight. The comparative weights of the different types of lines should be the same as in an instrument drawing. The information contained in the

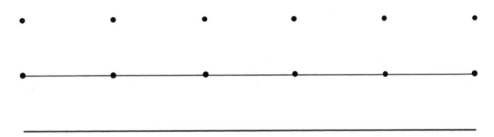

Fig. 8-1 Sketching straight lines

sketch should be complete. Most important, though measuring instruments are not used, the proportions of the object to be sketched should be reasonably accurate.

SKETCHING STRAIGHT LINES

Most of us can draw a short line free-hand and it will appear to be straight. Long lines, however, present a difficulty. No matter how we try, a long line drawn with a single stroke will appear wavy and bent. Repeated practice will improve the quality of line work. There are several tricks that the beginner can use to help in developing proficiency in drawing long lines. One trick is to use a series of dots along the path of the line to be drawn. To illustrate, draw a line freehand about 6 inces long. If it is drawn in one stroke, the line will almost certainly be wavy.

Instead of sketching the entire line, lay out a row of dots about 1 inch apart, figure 8-1. Now hold the paper up and sight along this row of dots. Any dot that is out of line shows up immediately and can easily be shifted so that all the dots are in line. To draw a light line connecting each of the dots is a relatively simple job. As a final step, go over the entire line with a single stroke, making it the desired weight. With additional practice, the beginner will be able to widen the distance between dots and, eventually, eliminate them entirely.

Horizontal lines are best drawn from left to right if you are right-handed, figure 8-2. Left-handed sketchers should draw from right to left. These lines should be drawn with a forearm rather than a wrist movement. While pivoting from the wrist may be a somewhat easier movement for the beginner, it will cause a curve when drawing longer lines. When a series of lines are to be drawn, it is a good practice to first sketch all lines lightly. When you are sure that your sketch is correct, the lines can all be darkened at the same time.

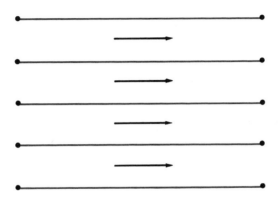

Fig. 8-2 Horizontal lines

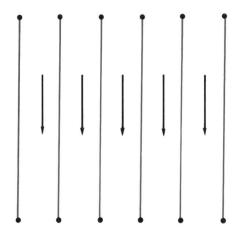

Fig. 8-3 Vertical lines

This eliminates much erasing and serves to keep the sketch clean.

Vertical lines are best drawn from the top down, figure 8-3. As in drawing horizontal lines, the forearm should be used as a pivot point. Long, vertical lines can be drawn by using the row of dots as an aid. To draw lines parallel, as they are shown in figure 8-3, is a difficult job for the beginner. Many people use a piece of paper as a ruler to mark off equal distances at each end of a line. A line sketched through these two points will be parallel to the first line. Again, repeated practice will increase the sketcher's proficiency to the point where the use of aids will not be necessary.

Sloping lines can be drawn in the same manner as horizontal or vertical lines, figure 8-4. An advantage of freehand sketching is that the paper is not fastened down in a stationary position, and the sketcher is free to turn the paper in any direction. This makes it simpler to draw lines that might otherwise be in an awkward position.

PROPORTION

Proportion is illustrated in figure 8-5. Assume that the object has the dimensions shown by the solid outline. If one side (A) of this rectangle is drawn to a larger scale, the other side (B) must be lengthened the same proportional amount. If side (B) were lengthened the same amount as side (A), the drawing would no longer be a true picture of the same object.

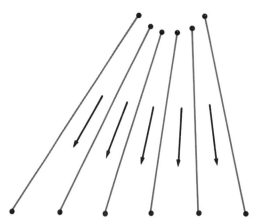

Fig. 8-4 Sloping lines

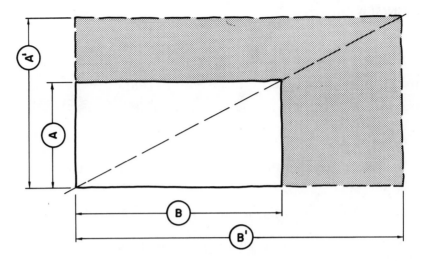

Fig. 8-5 Proportional sketching

The correct proportions are extremely important in freehand sketching. Since no measuring tools are used in freehand sketching, it is more difficult to show the accurate shape. The actual sizes used in a sketch are relatively unimportant. A line may be drawn two inches long and dimensioned five inches, but whatever unit of measure is used, the entire sketch must be made to that scale if the proportions are to be correct. Sketching an object freehand is not an excuse for distorting the proportions of the object.

Objects should be sketched in the same position as they appear, figure 8-6. The length and width of the drawing paper should conform to the length and width of the object to be sketched. Notes should be lettered so that they can be read from the bottom of the paper. Dimensions are read from the bottom and side of the drawing.

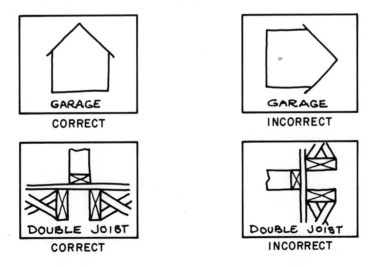

Fig. 8-6 Sketch objects in the proper position

ASSIGNMENT

A.   Sketching

Step 1 Make a complete two-view working sketch of the column footing.

Step 2 Show all dimensions.

Step 3 Make the sketch to a scale of 1 1/2" = 1'-0".

B.   QUESTIONS

1. What is the height of the straight (vertical) portion of the footing?
   _____

2. What are the overall dimensions of the footing?
   _____

3. How is a centerline distinguished from a dimension or extension line?
   _____

4. Will a third view provide any additional imformation on the footing?
   _____

5. Do all sides slope at the same angle?
   _____

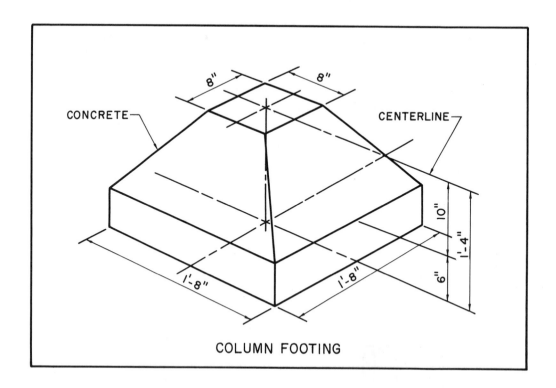

COLUMN FOOTING

ASSIGNMENT UNIT ⑧   DR.BY   CH.BY   RATING

UNIT 9 SKETCHING CIRCLES, ARCS, AND IRREGULAR SHAPES

OBJECTIVES

After completing this unit, the student will be able to:

- lay out and sketch small and large-diameter circles and arcs.

- lay out and sketch irregular shapes.

CIRCLES AND ARCS

Circles and parts of circles (arcs) are more difficult to sketch than straight lines. To simplify this operation, there are several techniques which can be used.

One of the main causes of poorly sketched circles is the fact that beginners try to draw the entire circle by sight and in one stroke. Like all other drawing details, a circle or an arc should be carefully laid out before it is drawn.

Notice that the circle in figure 9-1 bears some geometric resemblance to a square. Its length and height are the same size as are those of the square. If the square were circumscribed about the circle as shown, it can be seen that the two figures are tangent to each other at four points. These points are

the intersections of the centerlines of the circle and the midpoints of the sides of the square.

Since the square is relatively easy to sketch, it can be used as the beginning point for sketching the circle. The procedure for sketching a circle is as follows:

Step 1 Sketch a square of the same size as the diameter of the required circle.

Step 2 Mark off the midpoint of each of the four sides (A, B, C, and D).

Step 3 Sketch lines A-B and C-D. These lines represent the vertical and horizontal centerlines of the circle. They divide the square into four smaller squares, figure 9-2.

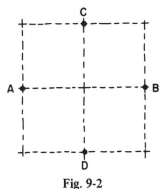

Fig. 9-2

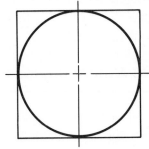

Fig. 9-1 A square circumscribed about a circle

Step 4 In each of the four squares, sketch an arc that is tangent to two sides of the square. Sketch these arcs with light, feathered strokes as shown in figure 9-3.

Step 5 When the four separate arcs have been sketched roughly, make any necessary sketching strokes to blend them completely into one smooth curve.

Step 6 Go over the outline of the circle with a single stroke so that the circle is drawn with the same line weight as the rest of the sketch.

SKETCHING LARGE-DIAMETER CIRCLES OR ARCS

The method outlined above is useful for the beginner in sketching small-diameter circles. Instead of working from a single reference point, the center of the circle, there are four such points to help in sketching a smooth outline. For large-diameter circles, however, four reference points are not enough to produce a smooth curve. The resultant circle, drawn with only four reference points, will usually consist of four flattened-out or otherwise distorted arcs.

The construction of a large-diameter circle requires the use of additional reference points which may be achieved in the following manner:

Step 1 Lay out centerlines A-B and C-D as shown in figure 9-4.

Step 2 Sketch in lines E-F and G-H. These diagonal lines should approximately bisect each of the four right angles which are formed by the two centerlines.

Step 3 Sketch in additional diagonal lines to subdivide all of the angles again as shown. Note: The larger the diameter of the circle, the more diagonal lines will be needed to produce a smoothly curved circle or arc.

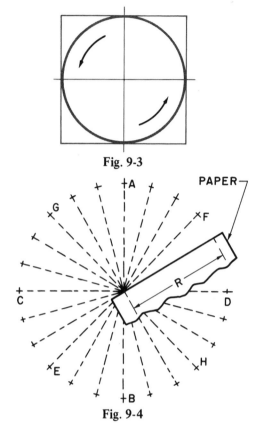

Fig. 9-3

Fig. 9-4

Step 4 Mark off the required radius from the center on each of the diagonal lines. To insure accuracy, the distance should be marked off on the edge of a sheet of paper and then transferred to each of the construction lines of the sketch.

Step 5 Sketch the circle with short strokes so that it passes through each of the reference points. Up to this point, all of the construction lines should be drawn as very light lines so that they will not interfere with the finished outline.

Step 6 Complete the circle with a solid, single-stroke line so that it blends with the rest of the sketch.

SKETCHING AN IRREGULAR SHAPE

Sketching an irregularly shaped object requires the use of many reference points. For such sketches, the use of graph paper, as shown in figure 9-5, greatly simplifies the drawing.

Figure 9-5 shows the steps to follow in sketching an object or a workpiece with a nonuniform or irregular shape.

Step 1 Lay out a series of equally spaced vertical and horizontal lines across the view to be sketched. The space between the lines will depend on the complexity of the shape. For the most accurate reproduction, the lines should be fairly close together. This condition will provide the greatest number of reference points.

Step 2 On a blank sheet of graph paper that has the same size squares as the origi-nal, plot each of the reference points as it appears on the original.

Step 3 Sketch in lightly the irregular shape so that it passes through each of the reference points.

Step 4 Darken the outline so that it blends in with the other lines of the sketch.

This method of sketching can also be used to make a sketch to a reduced or an enlarged scale. If the sketch is made on graph paper that has smaller or larger squares than the original layout, the finished sketch will be in perfect proportion to the original but will be either smaller or larger as desired.

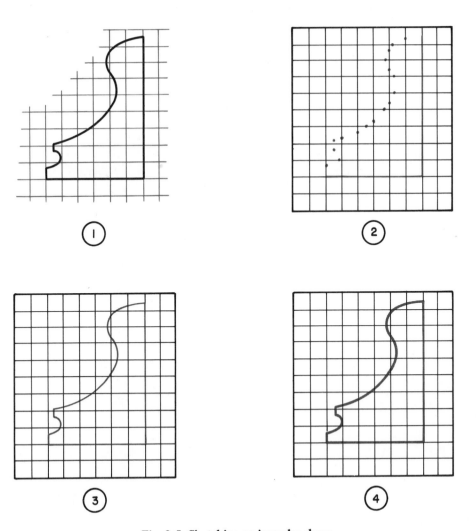

Fig. 9-5 Sketching an irregular shape

ASSIGNMENT

A. Sketching

Step 1 Make a two-view working sketch of the pipe chair. Make the sketch full size.

Step 2 Show all dimensions and centerlines.

B. Questions

1. What is the width of the base of the pipe chair?   _____

2. What is the height from the top of the base to the bottom of the 1″ radius?   _____

3. How far does the base project beyond the faces of the vertical members?   _____

4. Which two views will show the complete shape outline and all the necessary dimensions?   _____

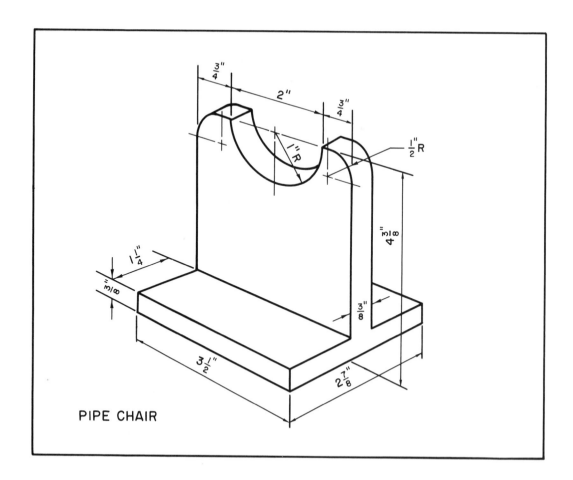

PIPE CHAIR

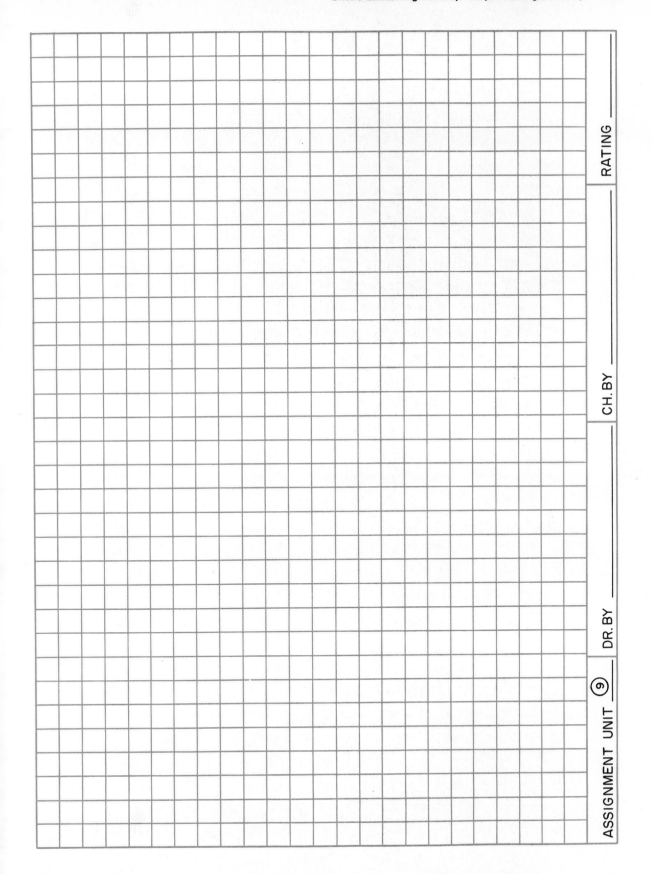

ASSIGNMENT UNIT ⑨   DR.BY   CH.BY   RATING

UNIT 10 MAKING A WORKING SKETCH

OBJECTIVES

After completing this unit, the student will be able to:

- plan a sketch.
- establish a systematic procedure for sketching.

On many repair jobs and small construction jobs, pencil sketches, rather than blueprints, are used as a guide. Making a blueprint requires the skillful preparation of a master drawing. These drawings are costly and take considerably more time to complete than sketches. It has already been pointed out that the working drawings, either blueprints or sketches, are used as a set of instructions. If a sketch is to be used, it should be neatly drawn, be complete in its information, and in approximate proportion to the actual size and shape of the job. By following a simple procedure, it is possible to systematize the sketching of any job.

THE BASIC RECTANGLE

Any object which is to be sketched, whether it is a single brick, a wall, a building or a molding, has a basic rectangular shape. Figure 10-1 illustrates how the size of this

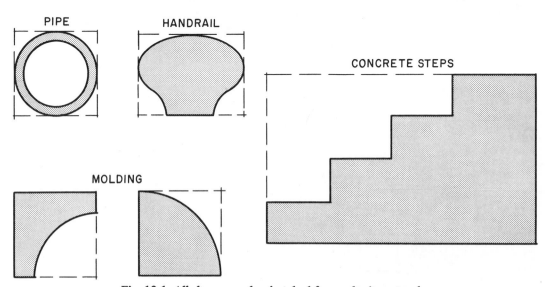

Fig. 10-1 All shapes can be sketched from a basic rectangle

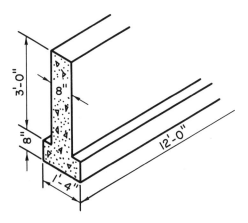

Fig. 10-2 Concrete wall and footing

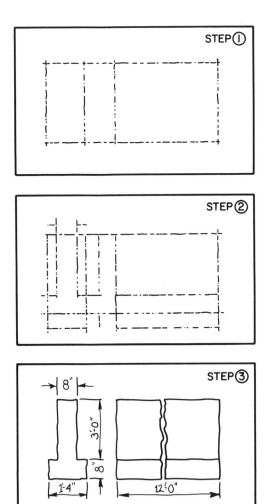

Fig. 10-3 Three steps in sketching

basic rectangle is determined from various sizes and shapes.

The importance of this basic rectangle is the fact that it is easier to sketch this simple figure and then complete the desired shape than it is to try to draw the irregular shape from the start.

STEPS IN SKETCHING

To make a working sketch of the concrete wall and footing shown in figure 10-2, first determine the number of views needed, the dimensions that must be noted, and the approximate scale or proportions of the drawing.

In figure 10-3, Step ① shows the rough outline of the two views that are necessary. Notice that the basic shape of these views is a rectangle. In making this rough outline, take care in the spacing of each view. Enough space should be provided between the views to include all of the necessary dimensions. The lines of the rough outline should be kept very light since they may have to be shifted slightly to obtain the proper proportions.

Step ② shows the lines which have been added to complete the shape outline in each of the views. Notice also that the locations of the dimension and extension lines have been added to these views. The lines are still kept very light to allow for changes and erasures.

Step ③ shows the completion of the sketch. The unnecessary lines have been erased. The extension, dimension, and object lines have been drawn to their proper weight, and the arrowheads, dimensions, and other necessary lettering have been filled in.

All the lines of the completed sketch should be drawn with single strokes. Going over a line two or three times makes it look ragged instead of sharp and clean. Drawing lines with single strokes is recommended because it is difficult to get even, straight lines with short, choppy strokes.

A sketch that is fairly simple and does not have many lines is sometimes faster to make if the guidelines are not erased. This means that these guidelines must be kept light enough so that they do not interfere with or detract from the sketch. For more complex drawings, it is a good practice to erase the guidelines before completing the sketch. This eliminates the possibility of darkening the wrong lines and then having to erase them.

Sketches should be completed by darkening the lines in a systematic way. A good procedure to follow is:

Step 1 Fill in the horizontal extension and dimension lines. Start from the top of the drawing.

Step 2 Add the vertical extension and dimension lines. Start from the left side of the drawing.

Step 3 Fill in the horizontal object lines. Start from the top of the drawing.

Step 4 Fill in the vertical object lines. Start from the left side of the drawing.

Step 5 Add the arrowheads, dimensions, and notes.

Following this procedure insures a minimum of hand movements over the drawing and helps to keep the drawing clean and free of smudges. In this procedure, the lightest lines are drawn first. The darkest parts of the sketch and the lettering are done last since they are most apt to smudge if a hand is brushed over them. For a person who sketches left-handed, the only change in this procedure is to fill in the vertical lines by starting at the right side of the paper.

ASSIGNMENT

A. Sketching

Step 1 Make a complete working sketch of the pipe tunnel.

Step 2 Make the sketch to a scale of 1/2″ = 1′-0″. Use a break line to fit the
12′-0″ dimension on the drawing sheet.

B. Questions

1. What is the outside height of the tunnel above the footings? _____

2. What is the height of the inside of the tunnel above the
concrete floor? _____

3. What is the width between the footings? _____

4. How many views are necessary to completely describe the
tunnel? _____

5. What is the width of each footing? _____

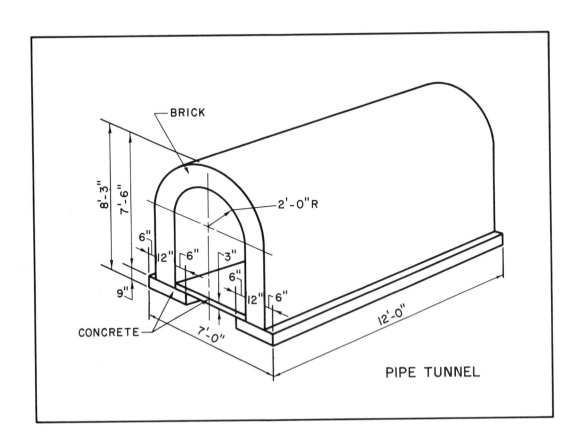

PIPE TUNNEL

RATING

CH. BY

DR. BY

ASSIGNMENT UNIT ⑩

UNIT 11 ISOMETRIC SKETCHING

OBJECTIVES

After completing this unit, the student will be able to:

- explain the principles of isometric sketching and drawing.
- Sketch rectangular shapes in isometric.

There are many construction details in a typical set of building plans that can best be explained or shown by using a pictoral drawing rather than orthographic projection. Several types of pictoral drawings have been developed for this purpose: isometric, oblique, and perspective drawings. These types are the most widely used for construction drawings, figure 11-1.

In each of these drawing styles the objective is not a flowery, artistic picture, but rather a drawing that shows shapes, locations, and

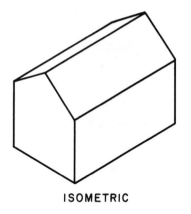

ISOMETRIC

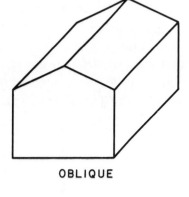

OBLIQUE

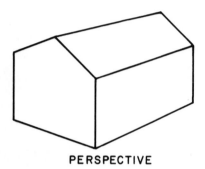

PERSPECTIVE

Fig. 11-1 Common types of pictoral drawings

dimensions of construction details. This must be done in a manner that is readily understandable to the workers who must use the drawings as instructions for the construction work.

The isometric drawing is one of the simplest types of drawings to make. It combines three views of the orthographic projection in a single picture, figure 11-2. By including the dimensions, this single sketch presents a set of instructions which are easy to follow and visualize.

To the construction worker who has an understanding of the orthographic form of trade drawing, the making of an isometric sketch or drawing is relatively simple. There are two basic rules to follow:

- Lines which are vertical in an orthographic elevation remain vertical in the isometric sketch.

- Lines which are horizontal in an orthographic elevation are projected at an angle of 30 degrees in an isometric sketch.

The word *isometric* means equal measure. In its application to drawing, it simply means that straight lines are drawn to their true length regardless of the fact that the views are projected at an angle. This removes the element of guesswork or judgment of the length of lines.

HOW TO MAKE AN ISOMETRIC SKETCH

The isometric sketch is started from three axes: the vertical axis which is common to the front and the end elevations (Line 1), and the two horizontal lines which represent the bottom surface of both of these views (Lines 2 and 3), figures 11-3 and 11-4. To make an isometric sketch of the notched block shown in the illustration, follow steps outlined below.

Step 1 Draw a light, long, vertical line to represent Line 1. Position it on the paper so that there is room for the rest of the sketch. Draw long, light guidelines to represent Lines 2 and 3. Draw these lines, representing the horizontal axes, at an angle of 30 degrees from the horizontal direction. To help estimate a 30-degree angle, remember that it is one-third of a right angle, figure 11-5.

Step 2 Mark off the overall height of the notched block on Line 1, the overall length on Line 2, and the overall width on Line 3 as indicated. Draw light lines through these points to complete the solid, rectangular outline which represents the basic shape of the notched block, figure 11-6.

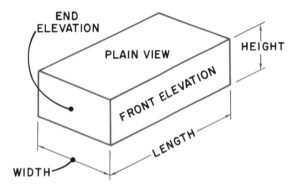

Fig. 11-2 Isometric drawing

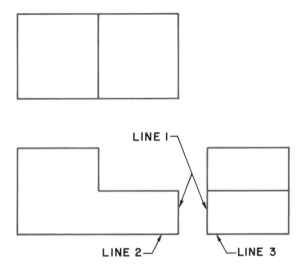

Fig. 11-3 Orthographic lines

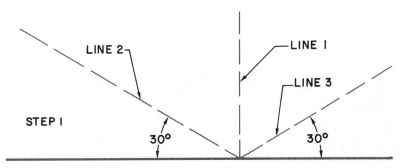

Fig. 11-4 Isometric Axes

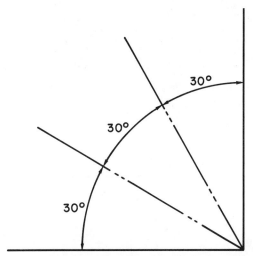

Fig. 11-5 30 degrees is one-third of a right angle

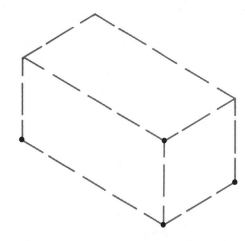

Fig. 11-6 Step 2

Step 3 Mark off the length and height of the notch on the lines of the front elevation. Through these points sketch in the vertical and horizontal lines of the notch. Project the ends of these lines as shown so that the surfaces of the

notch appear in all views of the isometric sketch, figure 11-7.

Step 4 Remove all unnecessary guidelines from the sketch and go over the outline with solid, single-stroke object lines.

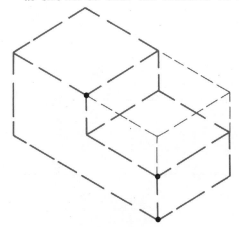

Fig. 11-7 Step 3

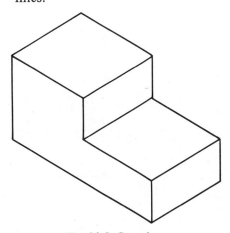

Fig. 11-8 Step 4

ASSIGNMENT

A.   Sketching

Step 1 Make an isometric sketch of the pilaster tile.

Step 2 Make the sketch to a scale of 6″ = 1′-0″.

Step 3 Omit all dimensions and hidden lines.

B.   Questions

1. What is the overall length?   _____

2. State the thickness of the horizontal center web on the
    front elevation.   _____

3. What is the overall width?   _____

4. What are the inside dimensions of each of the openings?   _____

5. Are all of the webs shown on the front elevation the
    same thickness?   _____

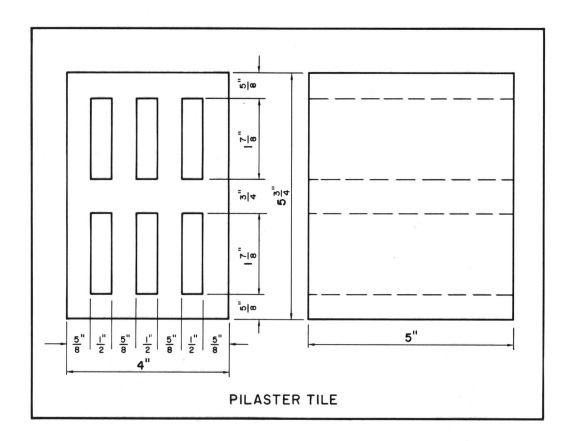

PILASTER TILE

ASSIGNMENT UNIT ⑪   DR. BY   CH. BY   RATING

UNIT 12 SKETCHING ANGLES IN ISOMETRIC

OBJECTIVE

After completing this unit, the student will be able to:

- make isometric sketches of objects with sloping or angled surfaces.

Since an isometric drawing is already projected at an angle to the viewer, the layout of any angular lines or surfaces cannot be done with a triangle or a protractor. This is because the drawing is in an orthographic projection. For example, if the 45-degree angle shown in figure 12-1 is drawn isometrically by

adding it to the basic 30-degree angle, the result is figure 12-2A.

If the 45-degree angle is measured from the horizontal direction, the result is figure 12-2B. In either case, the projection is a severe distortion of the chamfered block.

The proper method of projecting an angular line in an isometric is to determine the location of each end of the line, mark off these locations on the vertical and horizontal axes, then draw the line through these points. In the illustration there is a 45-degree angle on each end of the wood block. Note that in figure 12-3, page 70, the extremities of each of these lines have been marked off on the vertical and horizontal lines.

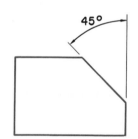

Fig. 12-1 Chamfered block

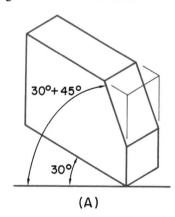

(A)

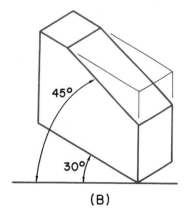

(B)

Fig. 12-2 Incorrectly drawn isometric

Remember that it is only the vertical and horizontal lines of a drawing that are drawn to their true length in an isometric. Angular lines are drawn either longer or shorter than in a flat view, depending on which side of the workpiece they are located. These lines, do, however, present the proper relationship to the other lines of the isometric drawing.

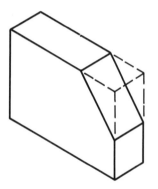

Fig. 12-3 Correctly drawn isometric

ASSIGNMENT

A.   Sketching

Step 1 Make an isometric sketch of the steel beam.

Step 2 Make the sketch to a scale of 6″ = 1′-0″. Use break lines to fit the 1′-4″ length on the ruled sheet.

Step 3 Omit the dimensioning.

B.   Questions

1.   What is the length of the beam?   _____

2.   What is the overall height?   _____

3.   What is the width of the flange?   _____

4.   How thick is the web?   _____

5.   Which lines in your sketch are not true length?   _____

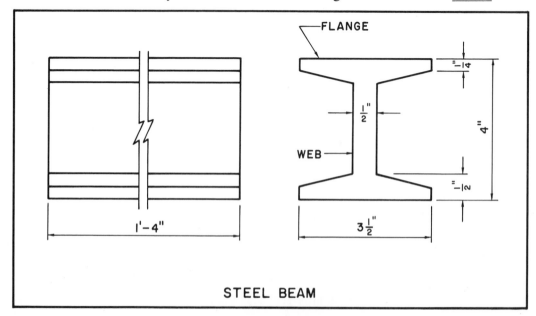

STEEL BEAM

ASSIGNMENT

⑫

DR.BY

CH.BY

RATING

UNIT 13 DIMENSIONING AN ISOMETRIC SKETCH

OBJECTIVES

After completing this unit, the student will be able to:

- read dimensions on isometric sketches.
- properly dimension isometric sketches.

The basic rules for dimensions on orthographic drawings apply to isometric dimensioning. Extension lines are continuations of object lines. Dimension lines are parallel to the surface being dimensioned.

The rule that horizontal lines are drawn at a 30-degree angle also applies to extension and dimension lines as shown in figure 13-1. Each of the extension lines is drawn as a continuation of the object lines. If the object line is vertical, the extension line is also vertical. For sloping lines, such as the 45-degree surface in figure 13-1, the extension lines are in line with the object lines. Straight dimension lines are drawn parallel to the surfaces being dimensioned. Angles are dimensioned with an arced dimension line.

There are no hard and fast rules for the location of dimensions in an isometric drawing other than those dictated by common sense. Careful consideration should be given to the location of dimensions before any of them are placed on the sketch. It is a good practice to keep all dimensions outside of the drawing itself whenever possible. Run extension lines only from the surfaces or lines that are visible, and avoid duplication of dimensions.

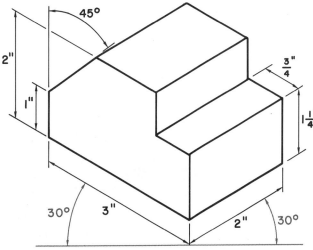

Fig. 13-1 Dimensioning an isometric drawing

ASSIGNMENT

A. Sketching

Step 1 Make an isometric sketch of the saw horse.

Step 2 Make the sketch to a scale of 1 1/2" = 1'-0". Each isometric square
of the ruled sheet will represent 2".

Step 3 Dimension the sketch completely.

B. Questions

1. What is the overall height of the horse? _____

2. What is the extreme length of the horse? _____

3. What is the extreme width of the horse? _____

4. How thick are the legs? _____

5. What is the width of the legs? _____

6. What effect will an increase have on the plan view of the
   horse? _____

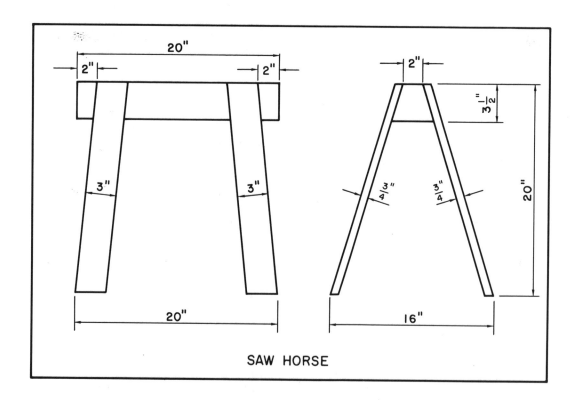

SAW HORSE

RATING

CH. BY

DR. BY

ASSIGNMENT UNIT   ⑬

UNIT 14 SKETCHING CIRCLES AND ARCS IN ISOMETRIC

OBJECTIVES

After completing this unit, the student will be able to:

- sketch isometric circles.
- sketch isometric arcs.

ISOMETRIC CIRCLES

Sketching circles in isometric requires some skill, but, with practice, smooth circles are possible. The sketcher must learn to judge the sharpness of curves. There are, however, techniques which make this easier.

The relationship between circles and squares was discussed in Unit 9. When a square is drawn about a circle, each side is tangent with the circle. The point of tangency (point at which they touch) is the midpoint of the side of the square, figure 14-1.

Isometric circles are normally shown in one of three positions, figure 14-2. The first step in sketching the circle is to sketch a square in the same position as the desired circle. Then, mark the midpoint of each side of the square,

figure 14-3A. The curved circumference of the circle is then sketched in four parts.

Notice that two corners of the square are *obtuse angles* (greater than 90 degrees). The opposite corners are *acute angles* (less than 90 degrees). The portions of the circle which are included in the obtuse corners have fairly large radii — slight curve. The portions of the circle which are included in the acute corners have shorter radii — sharper curve. To sketch the

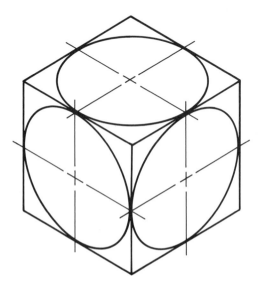

Fig. 14-2 Isometric circles are usually in one of three positions

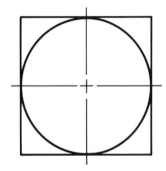

Fig. 14-1 Square about a circle

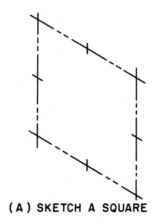

(A) SKETCH A SQUARE

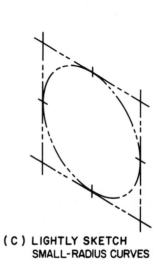

(B) LIGHTLY SKETCH
LARGE-RADIUS CURVES

(C) LIGHTLY SKETCH
SMALL-RADIUS CURVES

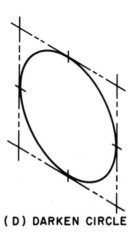

(D) DARKEN CIRCLE

Fig. 14-3

circle, lightly sketch the two shallow curves, figure 14-3B, then lightly sketch the sharper curves, figure 14-3C, and finally darken the lines, figure 14-3D.

ISOMETRIC ARCS

Since an arc is a portion of a circle, its isometric construction is similar to the construction of a circle. The procedure is the same, but only a portion of the circle is completed, figure 14-4.

The steps for sketching an isometric arc are:

Step 1   Imagine the arc as part of a complete circle.

Step 2   Lightly sketch an isometric square about this imaginary circle.

Step 3   Lightly sketch the portion of the circle which forms the arc.

Step 4   Darken the arc.

DIMENSIONING ISOMETRIC CIRCLES AND ARCS

Isometric circles are dimensioned along the isometric centerlines or outside of the drawing and parallel to these centerlines, figure 14-5. Because of their shape, the actual diameter of isometric circles is only shown along their centerlines. Measurements taken at any other position will be smaller or larger than the actual diameter.

In placing the dimensions on the drawing, the same rules are followed as in the construction of the drawing itself. The dimension is kept in the same plane as the view of the object. The extension and dimension lines follow the direction of the object lines to which they are related. Isometric arcs are dimensioned with a leader, as are orthographic arcs, figure 14-6.

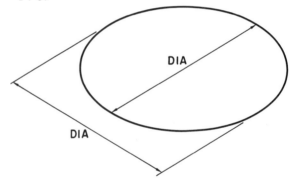

Fig. 14-5   Dimensioning isometric circles

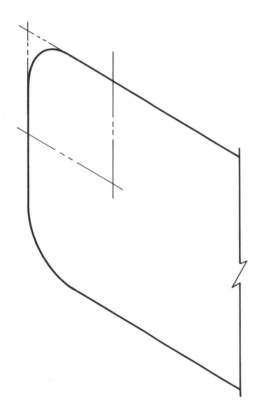

Fig. 14-4   Sketching an isometric arc

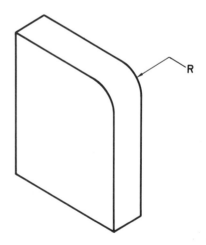

Fig. 14-6   Dimensioning isometric arcs

ASSIGNMENT

A.   Sketching Circles in 3 Positions

Step 1 Sketch an isometric cube with 2" sides (each square is 1/4").

Step 2 Sketch a circle on each face of the cube.

ASSIGNMENT UNIT⎯⎯⎯⎯⎯⎯ ⑭ ⎯⎯⎯⎯⎯⎯   DR. BY⎯⎯⎯⎯⎯⎯⎯⎯⎯⎯⎯⎯⎯

CH. BY⎯⎯⎯⎯⎯⎯⎯⎯⎯⎯⎯⎯⎯⎯⎯⎯   RATING⎯⎯⎯⎯⎯⎯⎯⎯⎯⎯⎯⎯⎯

B.   Sketching Cylinders

Step 1 Make an isometric sketch of the flanged bushing (1 square = 1/4").

Step 2 Dimension the sketch completely.

C.   Questions

1. What is the length of the 1" diameter?   _____

2. What is the length of the 2" diameter?   _____

3. What is the wall thickness of the bushing?   _____

4. What is the length of the 2 1/2" diameter?   _____

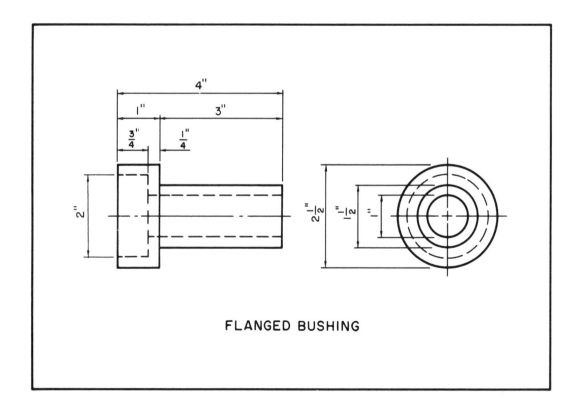

FLANGED BUSHING

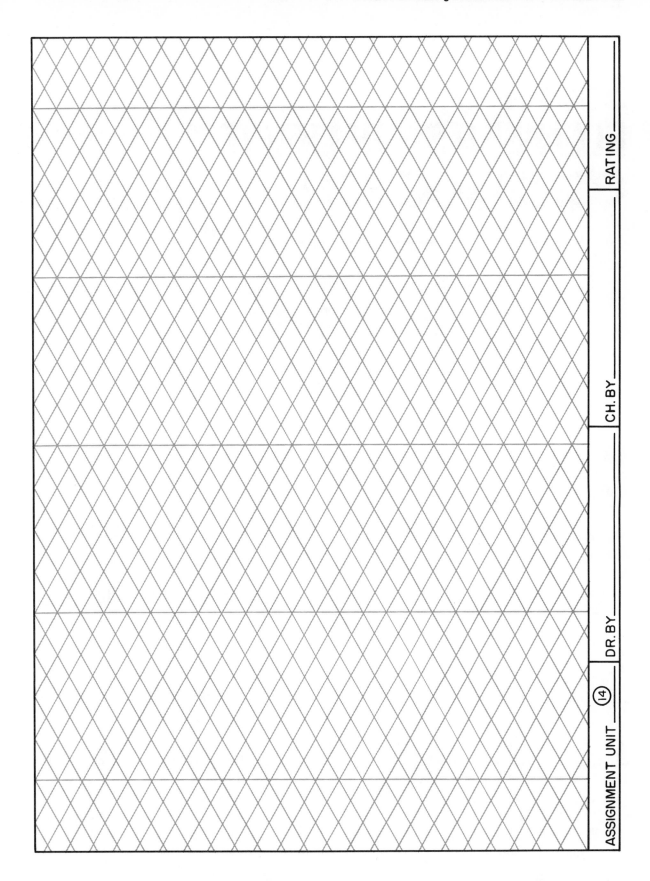

ASSIGNMENT UNIT _____ ⑭   DR.BY _____   CH.BY _____   RATING _____

Section 3
ELEMENTS OF LIGHT CONSTRUCTION

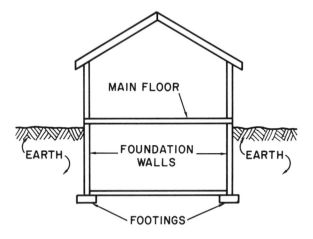

UNIT 15 FOUNDATIONS

OBJECTIVES

After completing this unit, the student will be able to:

- explain the functions of footings and foundations.
- identify the fasic features of a foundation.

PURPOSE OF A FOUNDATION

The foundation of a building is the portion below the first floor. The foundation for a building supports a heavy load. The heavier the building, the greater the load is on the foundation.

All of the weight of the building, including the foundation, eventually rests on the earth below. Very few types of soil are capable of supporting an entire building on the small area of a typical foundation wall. To spread the weight of the building over a larger area, the foundation walls usually rest on *footings,* figure 15-1. The footings are often about twice as wide as the thickness of the wall. However, the footing design varies according to the weight of the building and strength of the soil.

The depth at which the footings are placed is just as important as their size. Nearly

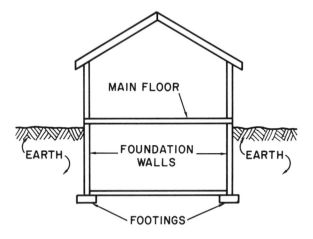

Fig. 15-1 Foundation

all soil contains water. As the water freezes the ground swells. The maximum depth to which ground freezes is called the *frost line,* figure 15-2. To prevent freezing and swelling from damaging the foundation, the footings must be below the frost line.

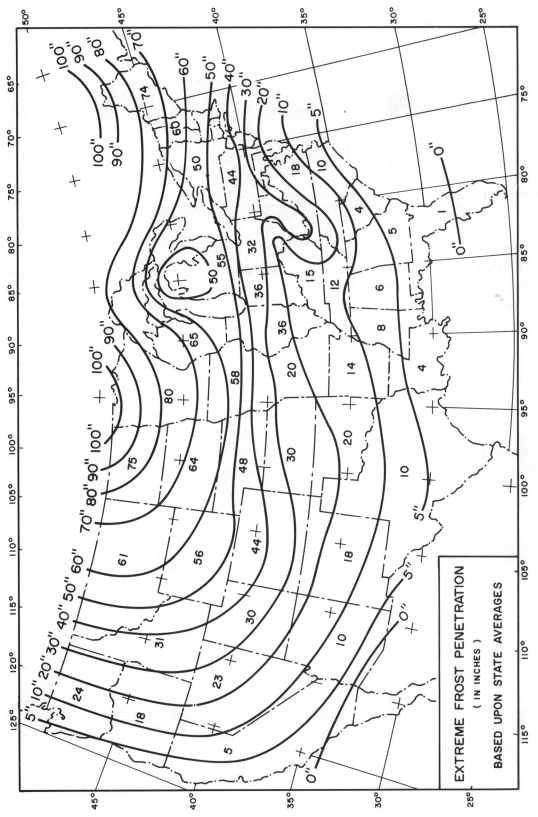

Fig. 15-2 Map showing average frost depths

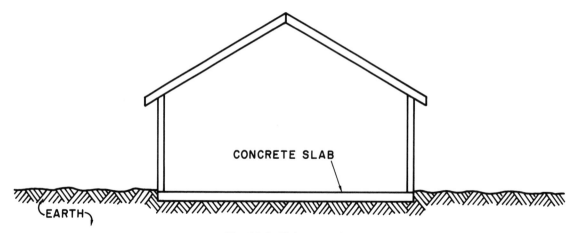

Fig. 15-3 Slab on grade

TYPES OF FOUNDATIONS

There are three types of foundations which are commonly used in small buildings. The simplest to understand is *slab-on-grade* construction, figure 15-3. In this kind of construction, concrete is placed directly on the ground for the first floor. Slab-on-grade (or *mat*) foundations distribute the building load over a very large area. However, this type is only suitable where the ground does not freeze.

Where the frost line is near the surface, the footings may be only a few feet below the surface. In this case, there is not enough space for a full cellar. Usually, however, a crawl space is provided for access to plumbing and wiring, figure 15-4. Crawl-space foundations are also used where there is too much ground water to make a dry basement practical.

In colder regions, the foundation is usually deep enough to allow for a basement. Houses with full basements usually have a water heater and furnace or boiler located in the basement. This design also includes cellar stairs.

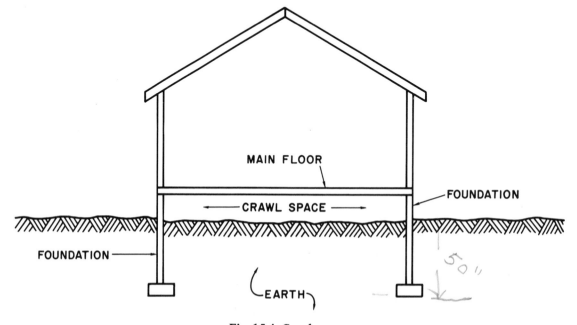

Fig. 15-4 Crawl space

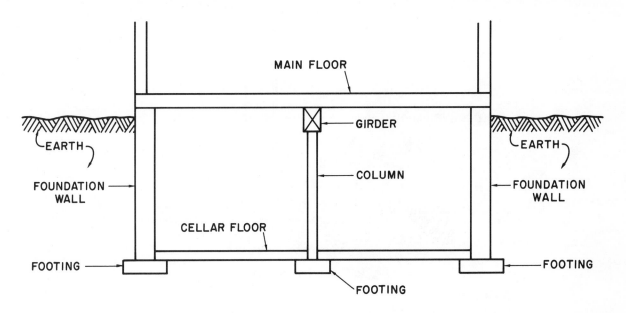

Fig. 15-5 Girders and columns support the floor between the foundation walls

COLUMNS AND GIRDERS

The floor of a building usually requires some support between the foundation walls. This support is provided by girders (wooden or steel beams) and posts or columns, figure 15-5. Girders may be *built up* by nailing several pieces of wood together, box beams made of plywood on a lumber frame, or steel, figure 15-6. The columns or posts which support the girder rest on concrete footings.

MOISTURE CONTROL

In all but very dry soil, some provision is made for keeping moisture out of the basement or crawl space. The most common method is to *parge* (plaster) the outside of the foundation with cement, then coat it with asphalt foundation coating.

As water passes through the ground and comes in contact with the asphalt-coated wall, it runs down the wall toward the footing. A plastic or ceramic drain pipe around the footing carries the water away from the building, figure 15-7, page 86.

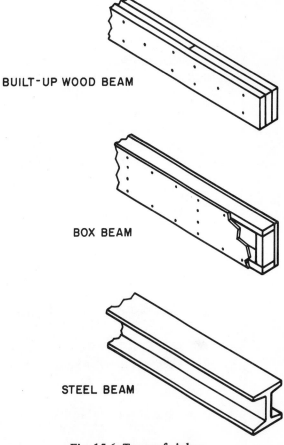

BUILT-UP WOOD BEAM

BOX BEAM

STEEL BEAM

Fig. 15-6 Types of girders

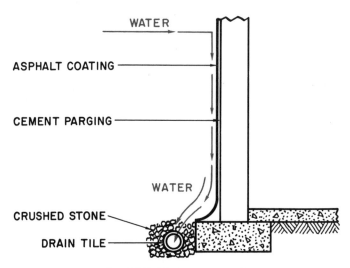

Fig. 15-7 Moisture control

ASSIGNMENT

Questions

1. What part of a building spreads its weight over a larger area of soil?

   _____

2. What is the most important factor in determining foundation depth?

   _____

3. What two factors affect the dimension of a footing? _____
   and _____

4. What is the name of the maximum depth to which the ground freezes?

   _____

5. Why is a slab on grade not practical for a house in the north? _____

   _____

6. What supports the floor of a house between the foundation walls?

   _____

7. What is the purpose of asphalt foundation coating? _____

   _____

8. When ground water reaches the footing, how can it be taken away?

   _____

9. When columns support a girder, what do the columns rest on? _____

   _____

10. Name three types of girders. _____

   _____

UNIT 16 FRAME CONSTRUCTION

OBJECTIVES

After completing this unit, the student will be able to:

- identify the basic parts in frame construction.

- explain the basic functions of the elements of a building frame.

THE ELEMENTS OF A BUILDING

The main elements of a building are the walls, floors, ceilings, and roof. In traditional frame construction, each of these elements consists of a frame and some kind of a covering. In order to fully understand a set of working drawings, it is necessary to know how the parts of each of these elements fit together.

FOUR-INCH MODULE

To understand the reasons for the size and spacing of many building materials, it is necessary to understand the *4-inch module*. Using 4 inches as a standard module, 4-foot wide building panels are exactly 12 modules wide, and 8-foot long panels are 24 modules long, figure 16-1. Some building panels are

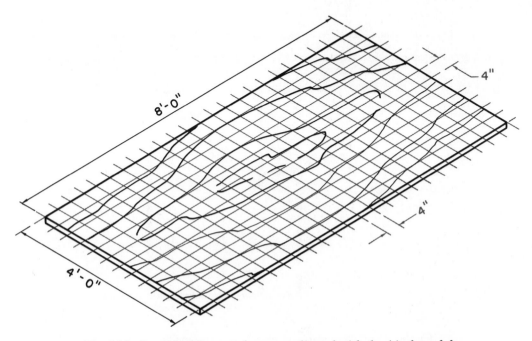

Fig. 16-1 4′ x 8′ building panels are coordinated with the 4-inch module

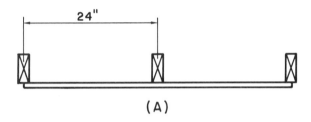

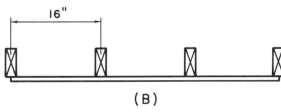

Fig. 16-2 Four-foot panels on 24-inch centers (A) and 16-inch centers (B)

manufactured in 2-foot widths, so they are 6 modules wide. Likewise, the length is often varied in 2-foot increments to conform with the 4-inch module.

Most building panels, such as plywood, gypsum wallboard, and particleboard, require support in three or four places for each 4-foot width. This requirement is easily accommodated by the 4-inch module. If framing members are spaced on 24-inch centers, 4-foot panels are supported in three places. If framing members are spaced 16 inches on center (OC), the panels are supported in four places, figure 16-2.

To avoid extra cutting and wasting of materials, buildings are generally designed

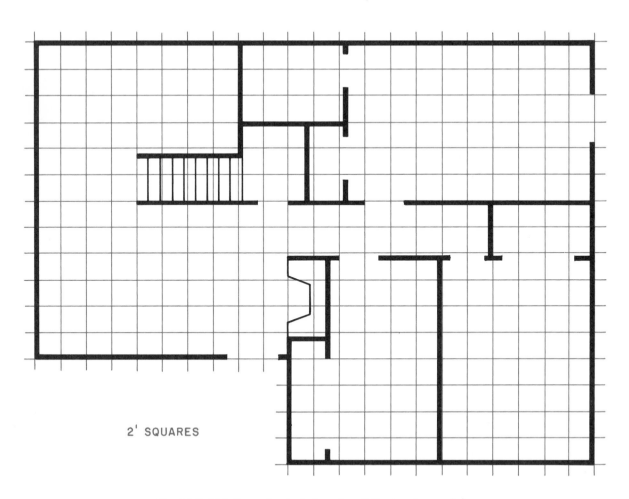

Fig. 16-3 This floor plan is designed on 2-foot major modules

around 24-inch major modules (six 4-inch modules), figure 16-3. Although it is not always possible to design rooms around the 24-inch module, the overall dimensions of the building are easily held to this standard. With this system, if a 2-foot piece of wall material (1/2 of a 4-foot panel) is leftover at one end of the wall, it can be used on the opposite wall.

WALLS

Walls serve two major functions. They separate spaces — one room from another or indoors from outdoors. They also support the weight of whatever is above then — second floor, ceiling, roof, etc. The *studs* in walls give them strength to support this weight. These vertical members are usually either 2" x 4" or 2" x 6" lumber. At their tops and bottoms, studs are fastened to *plates*.

Studs also provide a surface on which to attach covering materials. On the exterior, the wall covering is called *sheathing* and may be plywood, fiberboard, or foamed plastic sheets. On the interior, the most common wall coverings are gypsum wallboard and simulated wood paneling.

Additional framing members are used around the openings for doors and windows. A *header* is placed over the top of the opening. The header transfers the load from above the opening to the studs at the sides. These studs are doubled to carry the extra weight. In window openings, a stool is added to frame the bottom of the opening. Figure 16-4 shows the parts of a wall frame.

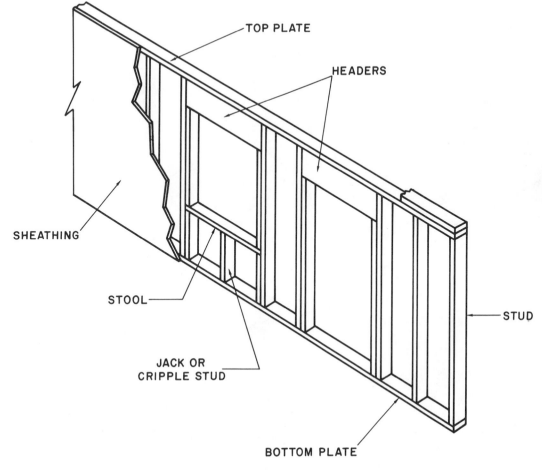

Fig. 16-4 Parts of a wall

FLOORS

Floors are similar to walls in that they are made of evenly spaced framing members which support a covering. In floors the framing members are *joists*. The joists rest on the foundation wall or a girder. The outer ends of the floor joists are joined by a *header joist*. *Bridging* is often added to prevent twisting and springiness in the floor joists. Bridging may be either diagonal pieces of wood or metal, or solid pieces of wood.

Where openings are made for stairs or chimneys, the joists are doubled and a *joist header* supports the ends of short joists.

Floor framing is covered with *subflooring* which is usually plywood. The subfloor is covered with hardwood flooring or underlayment. *Underlayment* adds strength which would otherwise be added by the hardwood flooring. Figure 16-5 shows the parts of a floor. Floors above the first floor are constructed the same, but rest on the lower frame walls instead of the foundation.

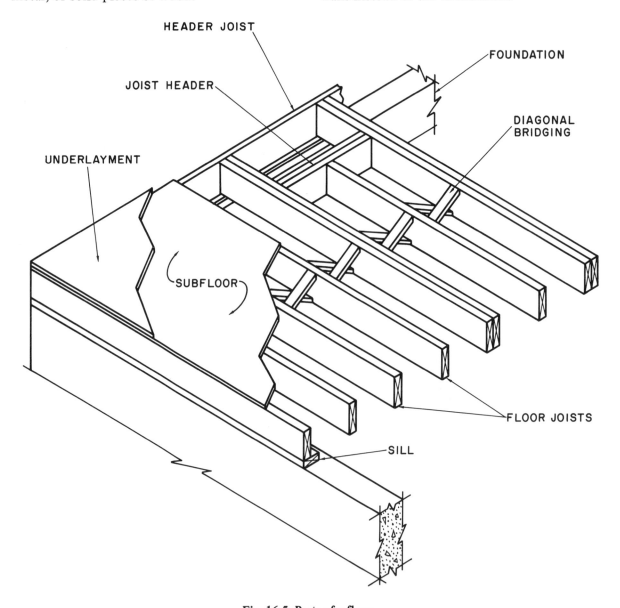

Fig. 16-5 Parts of a floor

CEILINGS

The ceiling is usually the underside of the floor above. In a single story house or the top story of other builidngs, the ceiling may be framed with smalller joists than a floor. Besides providing a surface at the top of the rooms, the ceiling joists prevent the walls from spreading apart.

ROOFS

A discussion of the main elements of frame construction would not be complete without including roof framing. The obvious function of a roof is to protect the building from the weather. Roof construction is explained in Unit 17. Figure 16-6 shows the relationship of the major parts of a building frame.

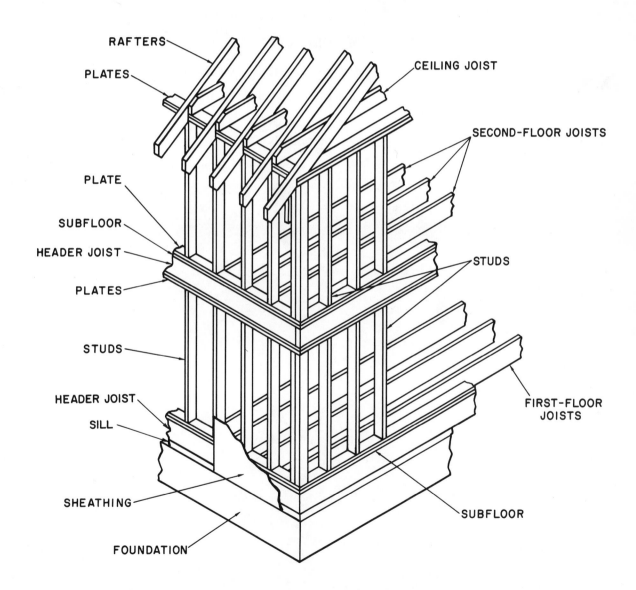

Fig. 16-6 Main elements of a house

ASSIGNMENT

A.   Matching

Indicate which of the building parts in the left-hand column is described by each item in the right-hand column.

a. Joist

b. Header joist

c. Stud

d. Bridging

e. Header

f. Subfloor

g. Top plate

h. Underlayment

i. Sheathing

j. Gypsum wallboard

_____ 1. Transfers the weight from above to the sides of an opening

_____ 2. Nailed to the ends of the floor joists

_____ 3. Nailed to the top of the floor joists

_____ 4. Main framing members in a floor

_____ 5. Main framing members in a wall

_____ 6. Diagonal bracing in a floor

_____ 7. Exterior wall covering

_____ 8. Interior wall covering

_____ 9. Applied over first layer of flooring instead of hardwood

_____ 10. Nailed to tops of studs

UNIT 17 ROOF FRAMING

OBJECTIVES

After completing this unit, the student will be able to:

- identify the most common types of roofs used on residences.
- explain the function of roof-framing members.

The roof of a house protects the structure and its occupants from rain and snow. The roof must be capable of supporting a heavy load, especially where several feet of snow may fall on the roof.

TYPES OF ROOFS

There are five types of roofs that are commonly used in residential construction, figure 17-1. Variations of these may be used to create certain architectural styles.

Gable Roof. The *gable roof* is one of the most common types used on houses. The gable roof consists of two sloping sides which meet at the ridge. The triangle formed at the ends of the house between the top plates of the wall and roof is called the *gable*.

Gambrel Roof. The *gambrel roof* is similar to the gable roof. On this roof, the sides slope very steeply from the walls to a point about halfway up the roof, then they have a more gradual slope.

Hip Roof. The *hip roof* slopes on all four sides. The hip roof has no exposed wall above the top plates. This results in all four sides of the

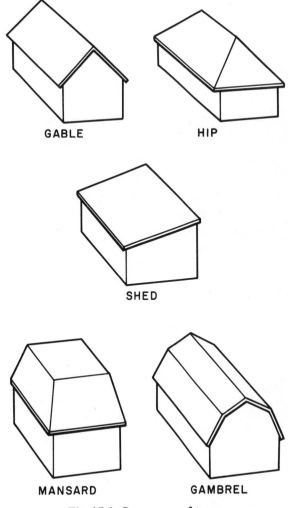

Fig. 17-1 Common roof types

house being equally protected from the weather.

Mansard Roof. The *Mansard roof* is similar to the hip roof, except the lower half of the roof has a very steep slope and the top half is more gradual. This roof style is used extensively in commercial construction, such as on stores.

Shed Roof. The *shed roof* is a simple sloped roof with no ridge. Although the shed roof is not as common as other types for residential construction, it is used on some modern houses and additions to houses.

CONVENTIONAL RAFTER FRAMING

The roof-framing members that extend from the wall plates to the ridge are called *common rafters*. On a shed roof the common rafters span the entire structure.

ROOF-FRAMING TERMS

The main parts in a roof above the ceiling joists are the rafters and the ridgeboard. The *ridgeboard* runs the length of the roof between the rafters of the two sides. The ridgeboard is a nailing surface for the tops of the rafters.

When the rafters are ready to be cut, the first one is carefully laid out and used as a pattern. To discuss rafters, a few terms must be understood, figure 17-2.

- *Span* is the total width to be covered by the rafters. This is usually the distance between the outside walls of the house.

- *Run* is the width covered by one rafter. If the roof has the same slope on both sides, the run is one-half the span.

- *Rise* is the height from the top of the wall plates to the top of the roof.

- *Measuring line* is an imaginary line along the center of the rafter. This is where the length of the rafter is measured.

- *Plumb cuts* are the cuts made at the top and bottom of each rafter. These cuts are plumb (vertical) when the rafter is in place.

- *Tail* is the portion of the rafter that extends from the wall outward to create the *overhang* at the eaves.

- *Pitch* is the steepness of the roof. This is usually expressed in terms of the number of inches of rise per foot of run. For example, if the height of the roof changes 4 inches for every 12 inches horizontally, the pitch is referred to as 4 in 12.

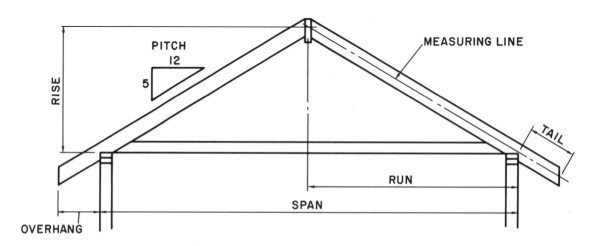

Fig. 17-2 Roof-framing terms

12	11	10	9	8	7	6	5	4	3	2
16 97	16 28	15 62	15	14 42	13 89	13 42	13	12 65	12 37	12 16
20 78	20 22	19 70	19 21	18 76	18 36	18	17 69	17 44	17 23	17 09
22 5/8	21 11/16	20 13/16	20	19 1/4	18 1/2	17 7/8	17 5/16	16 7/8	16 1/2	16 1/4
33 15/16	32 9/16	31 1/4	30	28 7/8	27 3/4	28 13/16	26	25 5/16	24 3/4	24 5/16
8 1/2	8 7/8	9 1/4	9 5/8	10	10 3/8	10 3/4	11 1/16	11 3/8	11 5/8	11 13/16
9 7/8	0 1/8	10 3/8	10 5/8	10 7/8	11 1/16	11 5/16	11 1/2	11 11/16	11 13/16	11 15/16

Fig. 17-3 Rafter table on the face of a square. The top line of the table is the length of common rafters per foot of run.

RAFTER TABLES

Carpenters use rafter tables to determine the length of the rafters. These tables are available in handbooks and are usually printed on framing squares, figure 17-3. To find the length of a common rafter:

Step 1 Find the number of inches of rise per foot of run at the top of the table. These numbers are the regular graduations on the square.

Step 2 Under this number, find the length of the rafter per foot of run. A space between the numbers indicates a decimal point.

Step 3 Multiply the length of the common rafter per foot of run (the number found in step 2) by the number of feet of run.

Step 4 Add the length of the tail and subtract one-half the thickness of the ridge-board. The result is the length of the common rafter as measured along the measuring line.

Note: If the overhang is given on the working drawings, it can be added to the run of the rafter instead of adding the length of the tail.

Example: Find the length of a common rafter for the roof in figure 17-4. (Refer to the rafter table in figure 17-3.

1. *Rise per foot of run = 4"*

2. *Length of common rafter per foot of run = 12.65"*

3. *Run of one rafter including overhang = 16'-0"*

4. *16 x 12.65" = 202.40" (round off to 202 1/2")*

5. *Subtract 1/2 the thickness of the ridge-board: 202 1/2" - 3/4" = 201 3/4"*

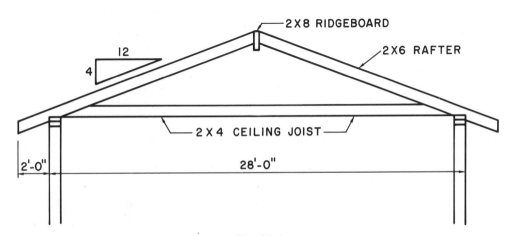

Fig. 17-4

TRUSSED RAFTERS

Through engineering advances, a system has been devised that speeds roof framing, reduces material needs, and produces stronger roofs. This is the use of trussed rafters. Trussed rafters, commonly called *roof trusses,* are units assembled in a shop. These units are then transported to the construction site and set on the walls, figure 17-5.

This is the system of roof construction used most often today. The top members of a truss, corresponding to rafters, are the *top chords.* The *bottom chord* is on the bottom of the truss and corresponds to the ceiling joists in conventional rafter framing. Depending on the design of the truss, there are several braces, called *webs,* between the top and bottom chords. The parts of the truss are held together with plywood or metal plates, called *gussets.*

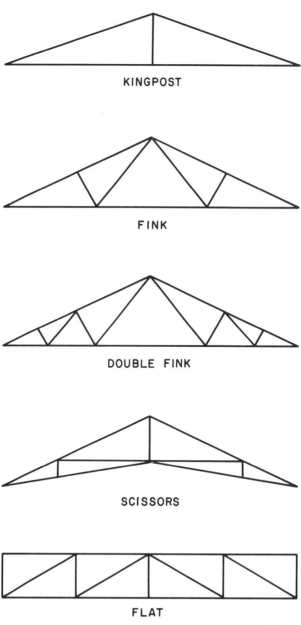

KINGPOST

FINK

DOUBLE FINK

SCISSORS

FLAT

Fig. 17-5 Some common types of roof trusses

GABLE FRAMING

Whether conventional framing or roof trusses are used, the triangular ends of a gable roof must be filled in with framing. If the architect specifies a trussed roof, gable trusses are set on the end walls. In conventional framing, gable-end studs are placed directly above the regular wall studs. Gable-end studs are toenailed to the top wall plate and notched to fit against the end rafter.

RAKE FRAMING

When the roof overhangs at the ends, special framing is required. This involves the use of *gable plates* and *lookouts*. The overhanging rafter is nailed to the ends of the lookouts. The lookouts rest on top of the gable plates, figure 17-6.

The final member of the roof frame is the *fascia header*. This is a piece of lumber the same size as the rafters nailed to the ends of the rafters. The fascia header will support trim to be added later.

ROOF COVERING

Most types of roof coverings require that the roof frame be covered with boards or plywood first. This is called the *roof sheathing* or *roof decking*. Roof sheathing is applied over the rafters in the same way that subflooring is applied over the floor joists.

The first step in covering the sheathing is to apply roofing underlayment. *Roofing underlayment* serves two purposes: It prevents chemical reactions between the resins in the wood and the roof covering material; and it provides additional weather protection. Asphalt-saturated felt is the most common roofing underlayment material.

Common roof coverings for residential construction are asphalt-rolled roofing, asphalt shingles, and wood shingles and shakes.

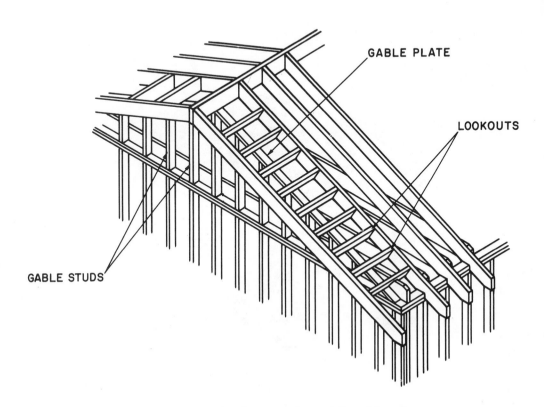

Fig. 17-6 Framing for an overhang at the gable end

Asphalt strip shingles are the most common. Asphalt shingles and rolled roofing are available in several weights. The weight is specified according to the weight of material required to cover one square. (A *square* is 100 square feet of roof.) Underlayment felt is generally a 15-pound weight. Strip shingles are generally 225- to 240-pound asphalt.

ASSIGNMENT

A. Identification

Show where these items are indicated in the illustrations of a conventional roof and a trussed rafter.

Top chord

Common rafter

Ridgeboard

Web member

Gusset

Gable stud

Bottom chord

Span

Tail

Fascia header

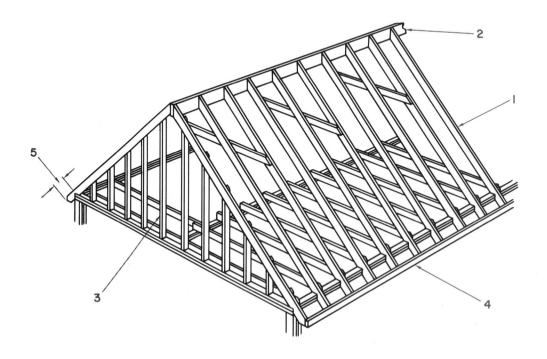

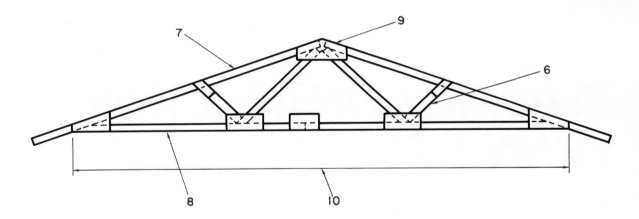

B.   Completion

1. The height from the top of the wall plates to the top of the roof is the
    _____.

2. The total width covered by a pair of rafters is the _____.

3. The width covered by a single rafter is the _____.

4. The imaginary line along which a rafter is measured is the _____.

5. The portion of a rafter that extends outside the wall plate is the _____.

6. The steepness of a roof is the _____.

7. A rafter which extends all the way from the wall plate to the ridgeboard
    is called a _____.

Section 4
READING CONSTRUCTION DRAWINGS

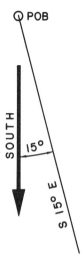

UNIT 18 PLOT PLANS

OBJECTIVES

After completing this unit, the student will be able to:

* identify features indicated on a plot plan.

* interpret boundary markings on a plot plan.

* interpret contour markings on a plot plan.

* interpret dimensions on a plot plan.

The work to be done on a building site and the location of the building is as important as the building itself. Before construction of the building begins, the site must be prepared. It may be necessary to add *fill* (soil) to low spots, remove it from high spots, and remove trees, etc. The plans for this work are communicated by use of a *plot plan*. The plot plan fully describes the site.

BOUNDARY DESCRIPTION

The first step in surveying a piece of property is to establish the *point of beginning* (POB). This may be called a *datum* or *bench mark* (BM). The point of beginning may be any stationary object, such as a manhole

Fig. 18-1 A line 15 degrees east of due south has a bearing of S 15° E.

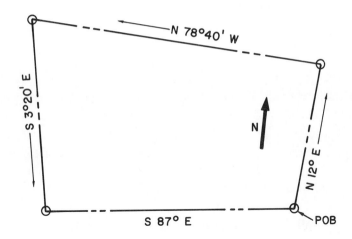

Fig. 18-2 Angles of less than one degree are given in minutes.

cover, iron pin, or existing building. The point of beginning is shown on the plot plan.

The direction and dimension of each boundary is measured from this point. A system of *bearings* is used to indicate direction. A bearing is given as a number of degrees east or west from a north or south line. For example, a line 15 degrees east of due south has a bearing of S 15° E, figure 18-1. Angles of less than one degree are measured in minutes (abbreviated by ′), figure 18-2. There are 60 minutes in a degree. A line 20 1/2 degrees west of due north has a bearing of N 20°30′ W.

CONTOUR

The height of a point is shown as an *elevation*. This is the number of feet above a particular reference point. The most common reference point for elevation is sea level, but it can be the surface of a nearby lake or a permanent monument erected by the city, town, or county. The elevation is given at each corner of the site, figure 18-3.

To describe the contour of the site, or rise and fall, a system of contour lines is used. These lines follow the surface of the land at a particular elevation. These lines are spaced at

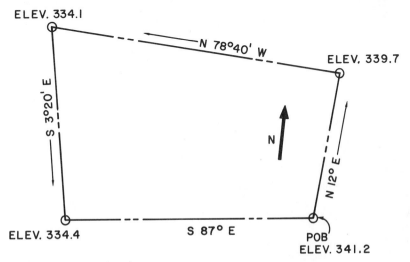

Fig. 18-3 The highest corner on this site is the point of beginning.

regular intervals of elevation, usually one foot. On a steep slope the lines are close together. On a gradual slope they are farther apart, figure 18-4.

If the contour of the site is to be changed, both the existing, or *natural* grade is shown by solid contour lines. The finished grade is shown by broken contour lines.

LOCATING THE BUILDING

The plot plan indicates where the building is to be located on the site. The basic shape of the building and its overall dimensions are given. The distances from the front and at least one side boundary are also given. In ad-

dition, the elevation of the first floor is included on the plot plan.

OTHER FEATURES

Anything else that provides useful information about the site is included on the plot plan. Walks, drives, and patios are shown with their dimensions. If there are other buildings on the site they are included. Trees are shown by symbols and any that are to be removed are marked. Utilities, such as water mains, sewers, and electric power lines, are shown by phantom lines. To help orient the plot plan, a bold arrow shows the direction of north.

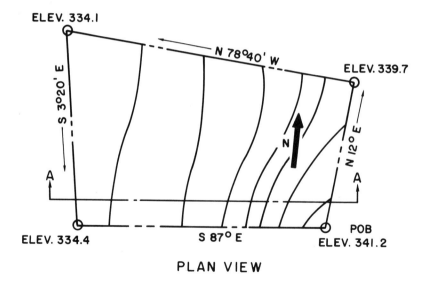

PLAN VIEW

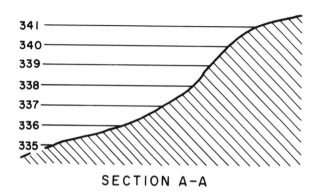

SECTION A-A

Fig. 18-4 The contour is shown with contour lines on the plot plan.

ASSIGNMENT

Questions

Refer to the drawings in the back of the textbook to answer the following questions.

1. What is the distance from the front boundary to the front of the house? _____

2. What is the length of each boundary line?

    North _____

    South _____

    East _____

    West _____

3. What is the highest elevation on the site? _____

4. What is the elevation where the walk meets the house? _____

5. What is the elevation at the northwest corner of the house? _____

6. How wide is the concrete walk? _____

7. What are the overall dimensions of the house, excluding the garage and terrace? _____

8. What utility services are available near the site? _____

9. At which end of the house is the slope of the site steepest? _____

10. What is the difference in height from the garage floor to the house floor? _____

UNIT 19 FOUNDATION PLANS

OBJECTIVES

After completing this unit, the student will be able to:

- identify features shown on a foundation plan.
- interpret dimensions shown on a foundation plan.

The foundation plan, like other plan views in construction, is shown as an imaginary cut through the foundation. It provides complete information for construction below the first floor.

FOUNDATION WALLS AND FOOTINGS

The foundation plan shows the dimensions of the foundation walls. The material of which the foundation is made is included in a note or by use of the proper section symbol. Most foundations are concrete or concrete block. Dimensions are included for the overall width and length, thickness, and the location of all features. Complete information about the location of intersecting walls and other prominent features is included, figure 19-1.

Some foundation plans show the footing with a hidden line. These plans may include a note giving the size of the footing. However, because local building codes often specify the size of the footing, the code should be checked in all cases.

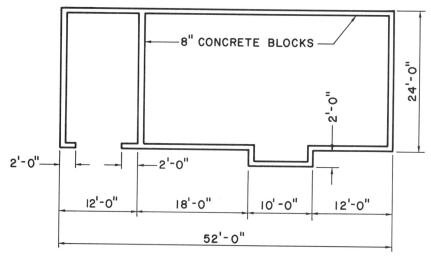

Fig. 19-1 Complete dimensions are given on the foundation plan.

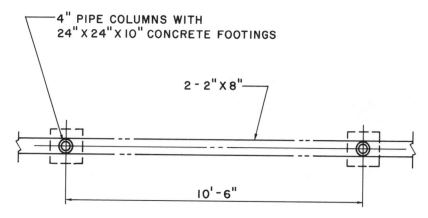

Fig. 19-2 Columns and girders are shown on the foundation plan.

COLUMNS AND GIRDERS

Most buildings include at least one girder resting on columns or masonry piers to support the first floor. These are shown on the foundation plan. Girders are shown by phantom lines with a note to indicate size and type. If the girder is supported by columns or posts, these are shown by a small circle. If the girder is supported by piers, they are shown by rectangles. In either case, their location is dimensioned to their centerlines. Each column, post, or pier rests on a footing which is shown on the foundation plan, figure 19-2.

FLOOR JOISTS

The size, direction, and spacing of joists is given on the plan for the space below. This means that information for the first-floor joists is shown on the foundation plan. This is customarily given by an arrow showing the direction and a note indicating the size and OC (On Center) spacing, figure 19-3. Where partitions above carry part of the weight of the building, the floor joists are usually doubled.

OTHER STRUCTURAL FEATURES

If the design of the building includes a cellar, the foundation plan includes stairs, windows, and doors. Some of these features may require more detail than can be shown on a typical foundation plan. Detail drawings which show this information are covered in Unit 22. However, the foundation plan includes dimensions for the location of these features.

Notes are included in any convenient uncluttered area to indicate such things as floor treatment and concrete slabs. Typical notes of this type indicate where concrete-slab floors are called for and where excavation is not required.

ELECTRICAL

The plans for houses and small commercial buildings usually include the location of electrical devices. The foundation plan may include light fixtures, switches, and the electrical service panel. These devices are shown by symbols, figure 19-4, page 106.

2"x8" - 16" OC

Fig. 19-3 This indicates that 2″ x 8″ joists are spaced 16 inches from the center of one to the center of the next.

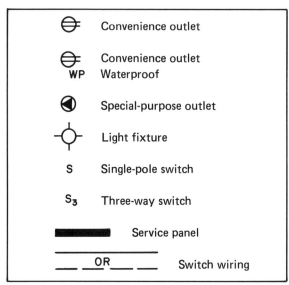

Fig. 19-4 Electrical symbols found on foundation plans

ASSIGNMENT

Questions

Refer to the drawings in the back of the textbook to answer the following questions.

1. What is the overall length of the house including the garage? _____

2. What are the overall dimensions of the garage? _____

3. How many 4-inch pipe columns are there? _____

4. What size (thickness x width) beams are used for the girders? _____

5. What is the main difference between the area on the right end of the house and that on the left end? _____

6. How many light fixtures are indicated? _____

7. What material are the foundation walls made of? _____

8. What size (thickness x width) are the first-floor joists? _____

9. What is the spacing of the first-floor joists? _____

10. How wide are the cellar stairs? _____

UNIT 20 FLOOR PLANS

OBJECTIVES

After completing this unit, the student will be able to:

- identify features shown on a floor plan.
- interpret dimensions shown on a floor plan.
- interpret information given in door and window schedules.

The floor plan is similar to the foundation plan. It is a section of the building at a height that shows the placement of walls, windows, doors, and other important features. A separate floor plan is drawn for each floor of the building.

WALLS AND PARTITIONS

Walls on a floor plan are drawn the same way as for a foundation plan. They are drawn to scale and their exact location is dimensioned. The location may be dimensioned from the centerline or the edge of the wall frame, figure 20-1. Because the carpenters who build the walls usually measure from the surface of the studs and plates, most dimensions are given from the surface of the wall frame.

DOORS

The location, size, and direction of opening (*swing*) are given for doors. Doors are shown on the plan with a symbol showing the swing. A straight line represents the door and an arc represents the swing of the outside edge. Other types of doors are shown by symbols which represent the operation of the door, figure 20-2, page 108.

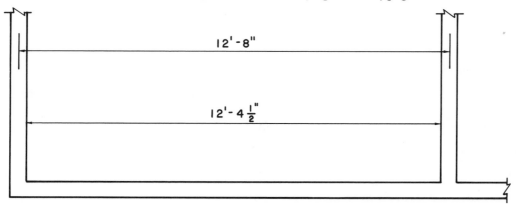

Fig. 20-1 Walls may be dimensioned to their centerline or their surface.

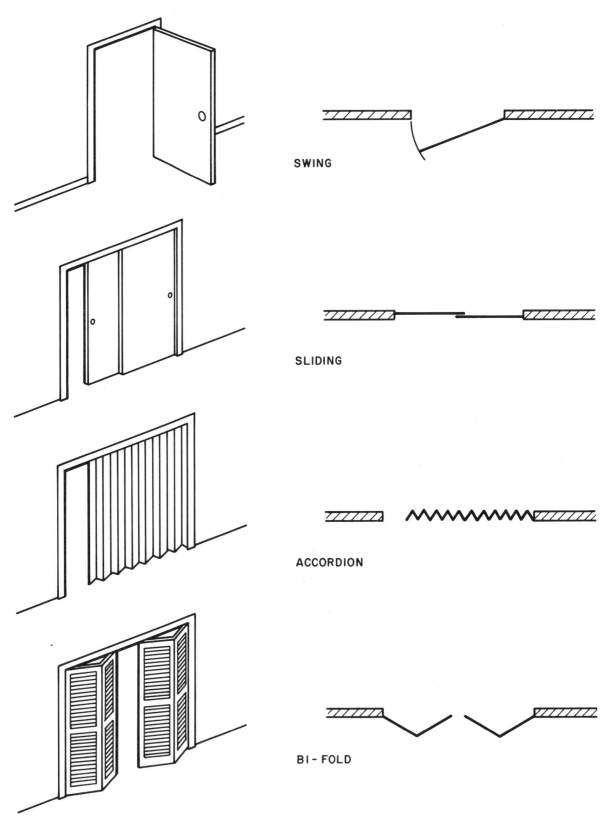

SWING

SLIDING

ACCORDION

BI – FOLD

Fig. 20-2 Types of doors and their plan symbols

Doors are generally available in widths from 2'-0" to 3'-0" in 2-inch increments. The height of most doors in homes is 6'-8", but 7'-0" doors are sometimes used for the main entrance. The width and height of the door is given either on the symbol or in a separate schedule.

Schedules are used to give information that would normally clutter the drawings. When a door schedule is used, doors are labeled with a letter or number. The schedule gives complete information for each type of door, figure 20-3.

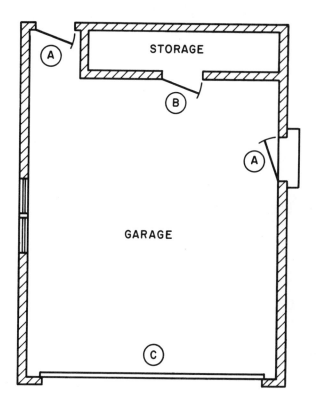

DOOR SCHEDULE

MARK	SIZE	TYPE	REMARKS
A	3'-0" x 6'-8"	2-PANEL	GLAZED
B	3'-0" x 6'-8"	FLUSH	SOLID CORE
C	18'-0" x 7'-0"	OVERHEAD	

Fig. 20-3

WINDOWS

There are basically five types of windows that are commonly found in houses and small commercial buildings. The plan symbol for each is shown in figure 20-4, pages 110-111.

The size of the rough opening (RO) into which the window will be set is especially important to the carpenter. However, the glass size and sash opening are also sometimes given, figure 20-5, page 112. The sizes for all windows should be checked with the manufacturer's catalog before the opening is framed. Window sizes are given with the width first and the height second. Information about the windows is sometimes given in a schedule.

In wood frame construction, the windows are located by a dimension given to their centerline. In masonry construction, dimensions are given to the edges of the opening.

OTHER FEATURES ON FLOOR PLANS

Plumbing fixtures. Plumbing fixtures are shown on floor plans by standard symbols. These symbols resemble the fixtures they represent. Plumbing fixture symbols do not include dimensions or other information. They are only intended to show the arrangement of the room.

Cabinets. Cabinets are usually included in the kitchen, bathroom, and laundry room. The outline of cabinets is included on the floor plan to show the general arrangement of these rooms. Special detail drawings (Unit 22) give the necessary information to install the cabinets.

Electrical devices. Electrical devices are shown by symbols in the same manner as on the foundation plan. These symbols do not completely describe the wiring of the house, but do show the approximate location of outlets, light fixtures, and switches.

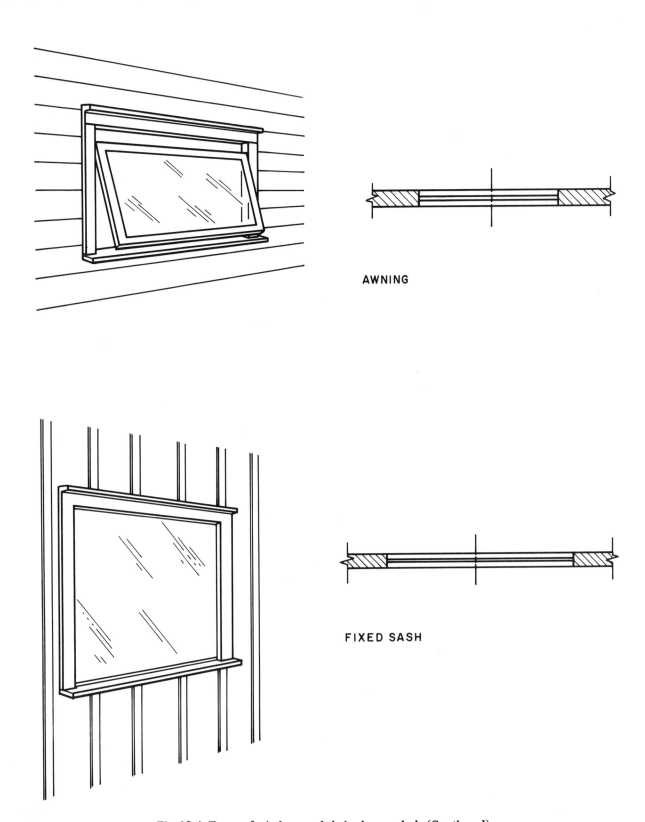

AWNING

FIXED SASH

Fig. 20-4 Types of windows and their plan symbols (Continued)

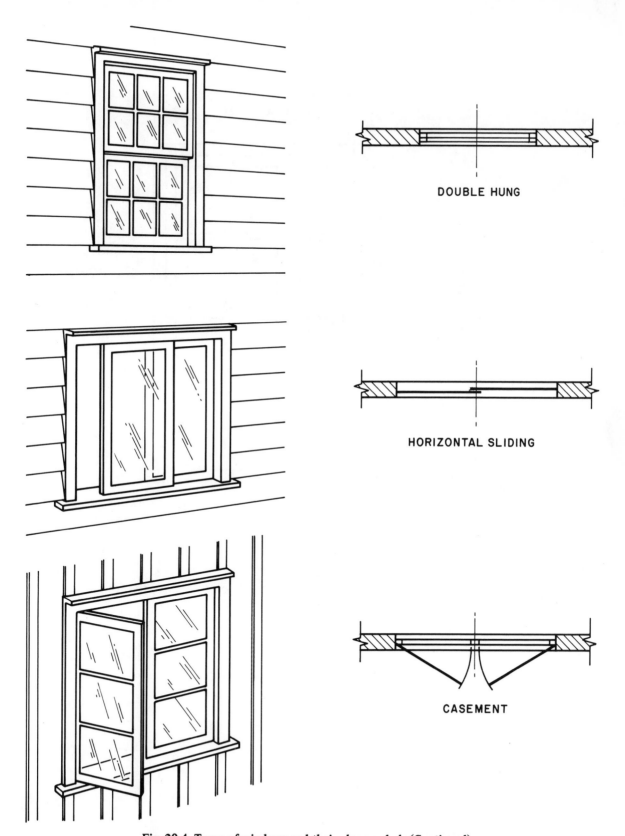

DOUBLE HUNG

HORIZONTAL SLIDING

CASEMENT

Fig. 20-4 Types of windows and their plan symbols (Continued)

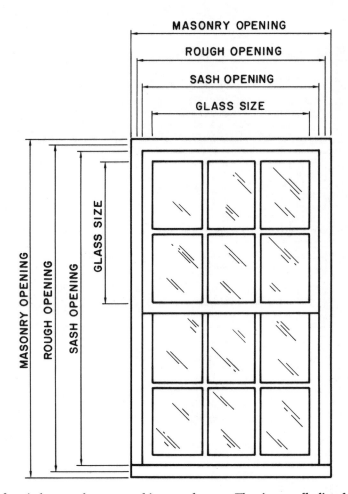

Fig. 20-5 The size of a window can be measured in several ways. The size usually listed is the sash opening.

ASSIGNMENT

Questions

Refer to the drawings in the back of the textbook to answer the following questions.

1. What is the overall length of the house including the garage?   _____

2. What are the inside dimensions of the garage? (Allow 4″ for walls.)   _____

3. What are the inside dimensions of the closet in bedroom #2?   _____

4. How wide is the overhead garage door?   _____

5. How many 3′-0″ wide windows are there?   _____

6. What size is the door at the head of the stairs?   _____

7. What is the floor area of the activity room?   _____

8. How many windows cannot be opened?   _____

9. How many light fixtures are indicated?   _____

10. How wide is the hallway from the foyer to the bedrooms?   _____

UNIT 21 ELEVATIONS

OBJECTIVES

After completing this unit, the student will be able to:

- orient exterior elevations to the building plans.

- interpret dimensions, notes, and symbols found on elevations.

- list information typically found on elevations.

GENERAL APPEARANCE

As was previously discussed, an elevation view is any orthographic drawing which shows the height of an object. However, when builders refer to elevations, they generally mean the exterior elevations of a building. A complete set of working drawings includes elevations of all four sides of a building. The elevations are labeled according to their position as you face the front of the building, figure 21-1.

Elevations are usually drawn to the same scale as the floor plans. The line work and symbols used are drawn to resemble the

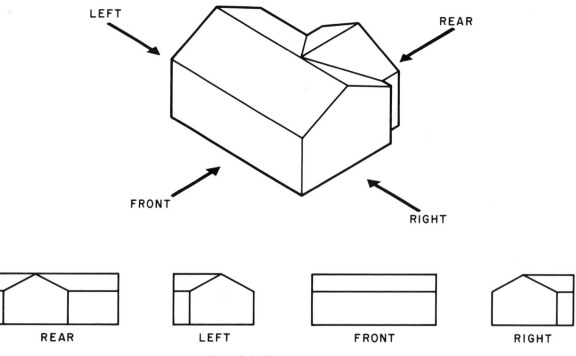

Fig. 21-1 Elevation positions

finished building. This allows the person reading the drawings to see what the finished building will look like.

Some architectural features are shown only on the elevations. For example, siding, masonry veneer, and roof covering are indicated by a note on one or more elevations.

FOUNDATION

The elevation drawings show the footing and foundation as hidden lines, figure 21-2. The foundation walls appear as vertical hidden lines. A rectangle at the bottom of the wall indicates the footing.

In some construction not all footings are placed at the same depth. For example, on steeply sloped sites, the footings are *stepped*

to correspond with the grade. This is necessary to keep all footings below the frost line. When a basement is combined with a slab on grade, the footings around the basement may be deeper than around the slab.

WINDOWS AND DOORS

All windows and doors are drawn to resemble their actual appearance on the elevations. Exterior doors are generally either flush or panel doors, figure 21-3, page 116. Flush doors are drawn with irregular lines to represent wood grain. Panel doors have rectangles representing the panels. Thin, short diagonal lines indicate glass, called *lites*.

Windows are also drawn as they actually appear. The size may be indicated on the

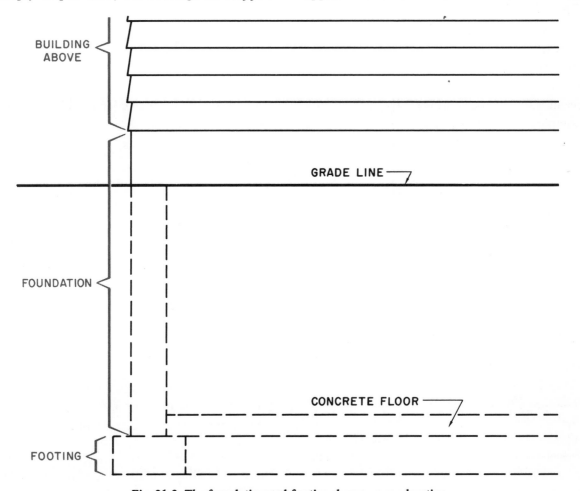

Fig. 21-2 The foundation and footing shown on an elevation

UNGLAZED   GLAZED

FLUSH

6-PANEL UNGLAZED   2-PANEL GLAZED

PANEL

Fig. 21-3 Types of exterior doors

elevation, but it is usually also included on the floor plan or a window schedule. The operation of the window may be shown on the elevations, figure 21-4. Sliding windows are indicated by horizontal arrows. Casement and awning windows have a dashed triangle. The point of the triangle is the hinged side of the window.

DIMENSIONS ON ELEVATIONS

Elevations have only a few dimensions — those that cannot be given on other drawings. The following are the dimensions included on most elevations:

Floor and ceiling heights. One of the elevations indicates the dimensions from the finished grade to the finished floor and from the finished floor to the ceiling. The finished grade is shown by a heavy line. The depth of the basement floor or footings is also given from the finished grade.

Window and door heads. Most doors are a standard height of 6'-8''. For uniform appearance, window heads are usually built at the same height as door heads. Because of this standardization, the height of window and door heads may be omitted. However, if any windows are to be set at nonstandard heights, the dimension from the finished floor to the window head (bottom of header) is given on the elevation.

Overhang at eaves. The amount of roof that projects beyond the walls is dimensioned on the elevations. This may not be the same dimension on all sides, so each elevation must be checked.

Roof pitch. The steepness of the roof is called the *pitch*. This is shown on the elevations by a triangular symbol. The pitch symbol includes two numbers. The number on the horizontal side, usually 12'', represents a unit of run. The number on the vertical side indicates the amount of rise.

Example:
For every 12 inches of run the roof rises 4 inches. This may be stated as 4 $\overbrace{}^{12}$.

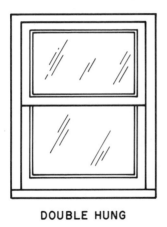

DOUBLE HUNG

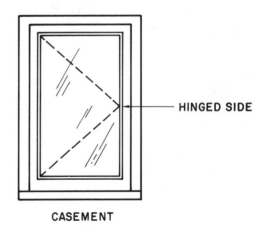

CASEMENT

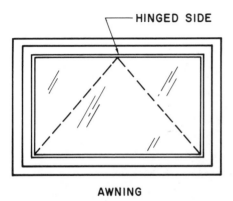

AWNING

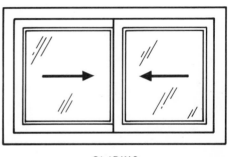

SLIDING

Fig. 21-4 Windows on elevations

ASSIGNMENT

Questions

Refer to the drawings in the back of the textbook to answer the following questions.

1. What is the pitch of the garage roof?   _____

2. Why is the footing under the right end of the house not as deep as the footing under the left end?   _____

   _____

3. What type windows are indicated for the main floor?   _____

4. Looking at the front elevation, the garage roof overhangs the right end of the house. How much is this overhang?   _____

5. How much headroom is there in the basement?   _____

6. How many windows are indicated in the basement?   _____

7. How many doors are shown on the elevations?   _____

8. What is the pitch of the roof over the front-left part of the house?   _____

9. What material is indicated for the foundation?   _____

10. In what part of the house are screened, louvered vents installed overhead?   _____

UNIT 22 DETAILS

OBJECTIVES

After completing this unit, the student will be able to:

- reference detail drawings to plans and elevations.
- interpret information given on detail drawings.

Not all of the necessary information about a building can be shown on regular plans and elevations. Objects which are too small to be drawn in complete detail on normal floor plans and building elevations are shown on large-scale detail drawings. Construction which is normally hidden from view is shown in section views. These large-scale and section drawings are called *details*. A set of working drawings usually includes several details.

REFERENCING

The first step in reading a detail drawing is to determine what part of the construction it shows. Details are used to show special construction that might not otherwise be understood. Some details may be labeled as typical. This means that the construction shown is used in several places in the construction project. Figure 22-1 is a detail of a typical door head. This construction is used for all sliding doors in the building. Most sets of working drawings include at least one typical wall section. When a section through the entire building is included, the wall section may be omitted.

Details that refer to only one place are identified by some mark on the drawing. As was pointed out in Unit 6, the section views are usually referenced by a cutting-plane line. This heavy line with arrows shows where the imaginary cut was made and from which direction it is viewed.

Reference marks for other details vary from one architect to another. It is important, although not usually difficult, to study the drawings and learn how the architect references details. One common method is with letters or numbers enclosed in triangles, figure 22-2, page 120.

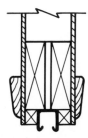

TYPICAL SLIDING DOOR HEAD

SCALE $1\frac{1}{2}" = 1'\text{-}0"$

Fig. 22-1

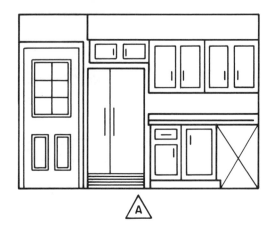

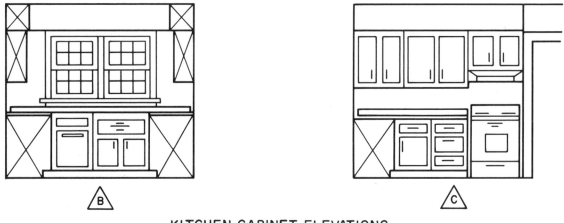

KITCHEN CABINET ELEVATIONS

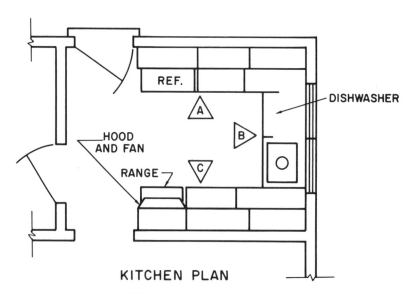

KITCHEN PLAN

Fig. 22-2 Each elevation is drawn as it would be seen by a person standing at the triangles on the plan.

SYMBOLS

Details must be clear enough to give the necessary information without confusion. One technique for simplifying section views is the use of material symbols. These symbols were discussed in Unit 7.

SCALE

Details are usually drawn at a larger scale than regular plans and elevations. Wall sections and other sections which show large parts of the building are usually the smallest scale of the details. They may be as small as $3/8'' = 1'-0''$. Details of small, complex parts are sometimes as large as $3'' = 1'-0''$, figure 22-3. Occasionally there may be a conflict between drawings. In this case, the largest scale drawing should be considered correct.

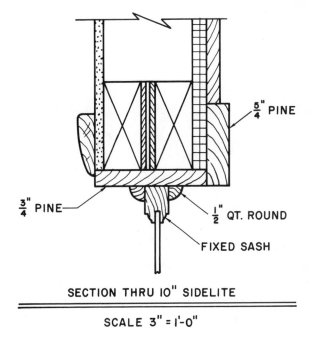

SECTION THRU 10" SIDELITE

SCALE 3" = 1'-0"

Fig. 22-3 Large-scale section view

ASSIGNMENT

Questions

Refer to the drawings in the back of the textbook to answer the following questions.

1. What is the height of the handrail above the stairs? _____

2. What size lumber is used to frame the stair landing? _____

3. What is the spacing of the roof rafters? _____

4. What is the size of the concrete footing? _____

5. What size sill rests on the foundation? _____

6. How much overhang is there at the eaves of the steep roof? _____

7. What is used for a header over the fixed windows at the top of the activity room? _____

8. What supports the top end of the rafters over the kitchen? _____

9. How many 24" wide x 36" high cabinets are required? _____

10. What is directly beneath the concrete slab in the basement? _____

UNIT 23 SPECIFICATIONS

OBJECTIVES

After completing this unit, the student will be able to:

- define specifications.
- describe the relationship between working drawings and specifications.
- interpret information found in construction specifications.

PURPOSE OF SPECIFICATIONS

When a set of working drawings for a building is made, it is impossible to include all of the information necessary to build the structure. For example, if the plans show wood floors, they might be oak, maple, or vertical grain fir. Tile flooring on the plans might be ceramic tile, asphalt tile, or vinyl tile. Where the plans show flashing, it could be galvanized steel, aluminum, or copper. Roof shingles can be asphalt or wood. The types of materials used and the quality of these materials must be described in some way.

Information that cannot be clearly shown on the drawings is conveyed to the builder by written specifications. The working drawings for a building give the shape, size, and location. Specifications describe the quality and type of materials, colors, finishes, and workmanship required.

The specifications become a distinct part of the contract. Once the contract has been signed, the specifications cannot be changed. Any corrections that must be made in the specifications after this point must be accompanied by a *change order*. In the case of a dis-

pute between the drawings and the specifications, the specifications should be followed.

Specifications are prepared by the architect or engineer and cover the entire project. The amount of detail and the exact form of the specifications may vary. Specifications serve several purposes:

- They make up a legal document that gives instructions for bids, owner-contractor agreements, insurance, and bond forms that are necessary.
- They help prevent disputes between the builder and the owner, or between the contractor and the architect.
- They eliminate conflicting opinions about the quality of the material to be used.
- They help the contractor estimate the material and labor.
- Together with the working drawings, they are necessary to complete the contract.
- Specifications are part of a legal document.

To make a complete set of specifications for each new job would be unnecessarily time consuming. Instead, specification writers rely on various references for standard specifications from which they compile a set for each new job.

DIVISIONS OF SPECIFICATIONS

In general, specifications for a residence are broken down into divisions that cover work by the different trades. It is standard practice to write the specifications in the order in which the house will be constructed. This makes it easier for the estimator to write a material list and for the contractor and subcontractors to locate specifications for their particular trade, material, or work.

The following are typical divisions of specifications for a residence:

General Conditions

Excavating and Backfill

Grading

Concrete

Masonry

Carpentry and Millwork

Sheet Metal and Roofing

Glass

Painting

Hardware

Heating and Air Conditioning

Plumbing

Electrical

GENERAL CONDITIONS

In order for the contract to provide complete protection to the parties involved, the specifications include General Conditions, such as the following:

- The contract form
- Supervision of the contract
- The architect's responsibility
- The contractor's responsibility for furnishing the lot lines and any restrictions
- Protection of the work in progress
- The following of manufacturers' instructions
- Quality of workmanship

This section usually mentions the fact that where manufacturers' trade names are listed, it is done to serve as a guide for quality and is not to restrict competitive bidding. Any work or materials not covered elsewhere in the specifications are normally covered in the General Conditions.

TECHNICAL DIVISIONS

Following the General Conditions, the specifications are arranged in divisions according to the work covered. These divisions are generally in the order in which the work is performed. They include all information about grade of materials, quality of workmanship, colors and finishes, etc., that cannot be shown on the drawings. A typical division of specifications follows.

DIVISION 6: CARPENTRY AND MILLWORK

A.   Materials

1.   All materials are to be the best of their respective kind. Lumber shall bear the mark and grade of the association under whose rules it is produced. Framing lumber shall be thoroughly seasoned with a maximum moisture content of 19 percent. All millwork shall be kiln dried.

2. Properly protect all materials. All lumber shall be kept under cover at the job site. Material shall not be delivered unduly long before it is required for work.

3. Lumber for various uses shall be as follows: Framing: No. 2 dimension, Douglas fir or yellow pine. Exterior Millwork: No. 1 clear white pine. The lumber must be sound, thoroughly seasoned, well manufactured, and free from warp which cannot be corrected by bridging or nailing. All woodwork which is exposed to view shall be S4S.

B. Installation

1. All work shall be done by skilled workers.

2. All work shall be erected plumb, true, square, and in accordance with the drawings.

3. Finish work shall be blind nailed as much as possible, and surface nails shall be set.

4. All work shall be securely nailed to studs, nailing blocks, grounds, furring, and nailing strips.

C. Grades and species of lumber

1. Framing lumber, except studs and wall plates, shall be No. 1 Douglas fir.

2. Studs, shoes, and double wall plates shall be Douglas fir, utility grade.

3. Bridging shall be 1″ x 3″ spruce.

4. Joists shall be spaced 16″ OC except where otherwise indicated. All joints are to be doubled under partitions and around stairways and fireplace openings.

5. Subflooring shall be plywood APA grade CDX.

6. Ceiling joists and rafters shall be spaced 16″ OC. Rafters are to have over-hang as noted on drawings.

7. Roof sheathing shall be 1/2″ x 4′ x 8′ plywood APA grade CD Exterior.

8. Moldings are to be clear pine.

9. Drywall material shall be 1/2″ thick gypsum wallboard.

10. Interior woodwork shall be kiln-dried clear pine. All interior woodwork is to be machine sanded at the mill and hand sanded on the job.

11. Hardwood flooring shall be 1″ x 3″ select oak.

12. Underlayment shall be 5/8″ x 4′ x 8′ particleboard underlayment.

D.   Workmanship

   1.   Framing: All framing members shall be substantially and accurately fitted together, well secured, braced, and nailed.   Plates and sills shall be halved together at all corners and splices.   Studs in walls and partitions shall be doubled at all corners and openings.   Joists over 8′ in span shall be bridged with one row of cross bridging, nailed up tight after the subfloor has been laid.

   2.   Gypsum wallboard: Gypsum wallboard shall be nailed to wood framing in strict accordance with the manufacturer's recommendation.   Space nails not more than 7″ apart on ceilings and not more than 8″ apart on sidewalls.   Dimple the nailheads slightly below the surface of the wallboard, taking care not to break the paper surface.

   3.   Interior trim and millwork: All exposed millwork shall be machine sanded to a smooth finish, with all joints tight and formed to conceal any shrinkage.   Miter exterior angles, butt and cope interior angles, and scarf all running joints in moldings.

   4.   Hardwood flooring: All subfloors are to be broom cleaned and covered with deadening felt before the finished floor is laid.   Wood flooring, where scheduled, is to be 1″ x 3″ T&G and end-matched select oak flooring.   Flooring is to be laid evenly and blind nailed or stapled every 16″ without tool marks.

   5.   Closet rods: Furnish and install where indicated on drawings.   Rods are to be adjustable chrome, fitted, and supported at least every 4′.

E.   Cleanup

Upon completion of work, all surplus and waste materials shall be removed from the building, and the entire structure and involved portions of the site shall be left in a neat, clean, and acceptable condition.

FORMAT FOR SPECIFICATIONS

The format or style in which specifications are written varies depending on the nature of the project and the specification writer. The example shown in this unit is typical of specifications for a small project. Most specifications for large projects follow the format established by the Construction Specifications Institute *(CSI Format),* figure 23-1, page 126. On very large projects there may be several hundred pages of specifications. Following the CSI Format makes the task of finding information easier.

On smaller projects a very brief form of specifications may be used. Figure 23-2, page 127, is a page of one style of brief specifications. Another common specification form is the Federal Housing Administration *Description of Materials.* This form is intended for construction to be financed by an F.H.A. loan, but is sometimes used for other projects.

DIVISION 1—GENERAL REQUIREMENTS

01010 SUMMARY OF WORK
01100 ALTERNATIVES
01150 MEASUREMENT & PAYMENT
01200 PROJECT MEETINGS
01300 SUBMITTALS
01400 QUALITY CONTROL
01500 TEMPORARY FACILITIES & CONTROLS
01600 MATERIAL & EQUIPMENT
01700 PROJECT CLOSEOUT

DIVISION 2—SITE WORK

02010 SUBSURFACE EXPLORATION
02100 CLEARING
02110 DEMOLITION
02200 EARTHWORK
02250 SOIL TREATMENT
02300 PILE FOUNDATIONS
02350 CAISSONS
02400 SHORING
02500 SITE DRAINAGE
02550 SITE UTILITIES
02600 PAVING & SURFACING
02700 SITE IMPROVEMENTS
02800 LANDSCAPING
02850 RAILROAD WORK
02900 MARINE WORK
02950 TUNNELING

DIVISION 3—CONCRETE

03100 CONCRETE FORMWORK
03150 FORMS
03200 CONCRETE REINFORCEMENT
03250 CONCRETE ACCESSORIES
03300 CAST-IN-PLACE CONCRETE
03350 SPECIALLY FINISHED (ARCHITECTURAL) CONCRETE
03360 SPECIALLY PLACED CONCRETE
03400 PRECAST CONCRETE
03500 CEMENTITIOUS DECKS
03600 GROUT

DIVISION 4—MASONRY

04100 MORTAR
04150 MASONRY ACCESSORIES
04200 UNIT MASONRY
04400 STONE
04500 MASONRY RESTORATION & CLEANING
04550 REFRACTORIES

DIVISION 5—METALS

05100 STRUCTURAL METAL FRAMING
05200 METAL JOISTS
05300 METAL DECKING
05400 LIGHTGAGE METAL FRAMING
05500 METAL FABRICATIONS
05700 ORNAMENTAL METAL
05800 EXPANSION CONTROL

DIVISION 6—WOOD & PLASTICS

06100 ROUGH CARPENTRY
06130 HEAVY TIMBER CONSTRUCTION
06150 TRESTLES
06170 PREFABRICATED STRUCTURAL WOOD
06200 FINISH CARPENTRY
06300 WOOD TREATMENT
06400 ARCHITECTURAL WOODWORK
06500 PREFABRICATED STRUCTURAL PLASTICS
06600 PLASTIC FABRICATIONS

DIVISION 7—THERMAL & MOISTURE PROTECTION

07100 WATERPROOFING

07150 DAMPPROOFING
07200 INSULATION
07300 SHINGLES & ROOFING TILES
07400 PREFORMED ROOFING & SIDING
07500 MEMBRANE ROOFING
07570 TRAFFIC TOPPING
07600 FLASHING & SHEET METAL
07800 ROOF ACCESSORIES
07900 SEALANTS

DIVISION 8—DOORS & WINDOWS

08100 METAL DOORS & FRAMES
08200 WOOD & PLASTIC DOORS
08300 SPECIAL DOORS
08400 ENTRANCES & STOREFRONTS
08500 METAL WINDOWS
08600 WOOD & PLASTIC WINDOWS
08650 SPECIAL WINDOWS
08700 HARDWARE & SPECIALTIES
08800 GLAZING
08900 WINDOW WALLS/CURTAIN WALLS

DIVISION 9—FINISHES

09100 LATH & PLASTER
09250 GYPSUM WALLBOARD
09300 TILE
09400 TERRAZZO
09500 ACOUSTICAL TREATMENT
09540 CEILING SUSPENSION SYSTEMS
09550 WOOD FLOORING
09650 RESILIENT FLOORING
09680 CARPETING
09700 SPECIAL FLOORING
09760 FLOOR TREATMENT
09800 SPECIAL COATINGS
09900 PAINTING
09950 WALL COVERING

DIVISION 10—SPECIALTIES

10100 CHALKBOARDS & TACKBOARDS
10150 COMPARTMENTS & CUBICLES
10200 LOUVERS & VENTS
10240 GRILLES & SCREENS
10260 WALL & CORNER GUARDS
10270 ACCESS FLOORING
10280 SPECIALTY MODULES
10290 PEST CONTROL
10300 FIREPLACES
10350 FLAGPOLES
10400 IDENTIFYING DEVICES
10450 PEDESTRIAN CONTROL DEVICES
10500 LOCKERS
10530 PROTECTIVE COVERS
10550 POSTAL SPECIALTIES
10600 PARTITIONS
10650 SCALES
10670 STORAGE SHELVING
10700 SUN CONTROL DEVICES (EXTERIOR)
10750 TELEPHONE ENCLOSURES
10800 TOILET & BATH ACCESSORIES
10900 WARDROBE SPECIALTIES

DIVISION 11—EQUIPMENT

11050 BUILT-IN MAINTENANCE EQUIPMENT
11100 BANK & VAULT EQUIPMENT
11150 COMMERCIAL EQUIPMENT
11170 CHECKROOM EQUIPMENT
11180 DARKROOM EQUIPMENT
11200 ECCLESIASTICAL EQUIPMENT
11300 EDUCATIONAL EQUIPMENT
11400 FOOD SERVICE EQUIPMENT
11480 VENDING EQUIPMENT
11500 ATHLETIC EQUIPMENT
11550 INDUSTRIAL EQUIPMENT
11600 LABORATORY EQUIPMENT
11630 LAUNDRY EQUIPMENT
11650 LIBRARY EQUIPMENT

11700 MEDICAL EQUIPMENT
11800 MORTUARY EQUIPMENT
11830 MUSICAL EQUIPMENT
11850 PARKING EQUIPMENT
11860 WASTE HANDLING EQUIPMENT
11870 LOADING DOCK EQUIPMENT
11880 DETENTION EQUIPMENT
11900 RESIDENTIAL EQUIPMENT
11970 THEATER & STAGE EQUIPMENT
11990 REGISTRATION EQUIPMENT

DIVISION 12—FURNISHINGS

12100 ARTWORK
12300 CABINETS & STORAGE
12500 WINDOW TREATMENT
12550 FABRICS
12600 FURNITURE
12670 RUGS & MATS
12700 SEATING
12800 FURNISHING ACCESSORIES

DIVISION 13—SPECIAL CONSTRUCTION

13010 AIR SUPPORTED STRUCTURES
13050 INTEGRATED ASSEMBLIES
13100 AUDIOMETRIC ROOM
13250 CLEAN ROOM
13350 HYPERBARIC ROOM
13400 INCINERATORS
13440 INSTRUMENTATION
13450 INSULATED ROOM
13500 INTEGRATED CEILING
13540 NUCLEAR REACTORS
13550 OBSERVATORY
13600 PREFABRICATED STRUCTURES
13700 SPECIAL PURPOSE ROOMS & BUILDINGS
13750 RADIATION PROTECTION
13770 SOUND & VIBRATION CONTROL
13800 VAULTS
13850 SWIMMING POOLS

DIVISION 14—CONVEYING SYSTEMS

14100 DUMBWAITERS
14200 ELEVATORS
14300 HOISTS & CRANES
14400 LIFTS
14500 MATERIAL HANDLING SYSTEMS
14570 TURNTABLES
14600 MOVING STAIRS & WALKS
14700 TUBE SYSTEMS
14800 POWERED SCAFFOLDING

DIVISION 15—MECHANICAL

15010 GENERAL PROVISIONS
15050 BASIC MATERIALS & METHODS
15180 INSULATION
15200 WATER SUPPLY & TREATMENT
15300 WASTE WATER DISPOSAL & TREATMENT
15400 PLUMBING
15500 FIRE PROTECTION
15600 POWER OR HEAT GENERATION
15650 REFRIGERATION
15700 LIQUID HEAT TRANSFER
15800 AIR DISTRIBUTION
15900 CONTROLS & INSTRUMENTATION

DIVISION 16—ELECTRICAL

16010 GENERAL PROVISIONS
16100 BASIC MATERIALS & METHODS
16200 POWER GENERATION
16300 POWER TRANSMISSION
16400 SERVICE & DISTRIBUTION
16500 LIGHTING
16600 SPECIAL SYSTEMS
16700 COMMUNICATIONS
16850 HEATING & COOLING
16900 CONTROLS & INSTRUMENTATION

Fig. 23-1 CSI format for specifications

SHEATHING

Outside walls shall be covered with . . . .

securely nailed. Roof sheathing shall be of . . . .

. . . .

securely nailed to rafters.

SIDINGS

Siding, if any, to be . . . .

ROOFING

Shingles for roof to be . . . .

laid . . . . .inches to weather using galvanized nails.

SIDEWALL SHINGLES

Sidewall shingles, if any, to be . . . .

. . . .

INSULATION AND PAPER

Sidewall insulation to be . . . .

Top floor ceiling insulation to be . . . .

Building paper under shingles to be . . . .

Building paper over sheathing to be . . . .

Building paper between subfloor and finish floor to be . . . .

OUTSIDE FINISH

All lumber required for outside finish shall be . . . .

. . . .

WINDOW AND DOOR FRAMES

All window and outside door frames as shown on plans shall be of sound clear pine, free from objectionable

defects. Outside casings . . . . .thick. Door sills shall be. . . . .

Assembled basement sash units, if any, shall be . . . .

Assembled window units, if any, shall be . . . .

Assembled door units, if any, shall be . . . .

Fig. 23-2 Brief form of specifications

ASSIGNMENT

Questions

Refer to the specifications in the back of the textbook to answer the following questions.

1. What size lumber is used for the wood sills resting on the foundation?   _____

2. What material is used for the piers on the porch?   _____

3. How thick is the gravel fill under the basement floor?   _____

4. What grade or weight of aluminum is to be used for the aluminum flashing around the chimney?   _____

5. How is exterior trim to be finished?   _____

6. What is the material and thickness for the stair treads?   _____

7. What color is the kitchen floor?   _____

8. How much money is allowed for light fixtures?   _____

9. What company is specified as the manufacturer of the overhead fixed-sash windows?   _____

10. How thick is the insulation under the basement floor?   _____

INDEX

The packet attached to the back cover contains 6 drawings and specifications.

1— Plot Plan
2— Foundation Plan
3— Floor Plan
4— Front Elevation and Rear Elevation
5— Right Elevation and Left Elevation
6— Details
7— Specifications